PAGES FROM A JOURNAL

PAGES
FROM
A
JOURNAL

By
Joyce Butler

Illustrated By
Steve Hrehovcik

Foreword By
Alexander B. Brook

Mercer House Press
Kennebunkport, Maine

Library of Congress Number: 76-685

International Standard Book Number: 0-89080-006-5

Acknowledgements:

The quotation from W.H. Auden is reprinted by permission of Random House from the book *Epistle to a Godson and Other Poems*, 1972.

The essay "Jamie's Autobiography" is reprinted by permission of the *Christian Science Monitor*, Copyright 1972, The Christian Science Publishing Society. All rights reserved.

Manufactured in the United States of America.

MERCER
HOUSE
PRESS **P.O. BOX 681**

**KENNEBUNKPORT, ME
04046**

For G.R.B.
because

Let us hymn the small but journal
wonders of Nature and of households . . .
W. H. Auden
Epistle To A Godson

Joyce Butler first came to see me with her desire to write a personal column for the *York County Coast Star* before Christmas, 1967. On January 3rd, 1968, the first piece appeared under her "Pages From A Journal" logo. In the 380 or so weeks and many columns since then her children have grown from 6, 8, and 10 to 13, 15, and 17. Sixty-five of the pieces written during the first three of those years have been chosen for this book.

Maine abounds in people who like to write, natural writers who set things down because they like to give artistry and permanence to their thoughts, and Joyce was one of these. Whether Maine grows such people or attracts them, and why, might itself be a Joyce Butler column subject. While most of these writers are either relatively unprofessional (soon tiring), or professionally flamboyant (flashing in the pan), Joyce has been sustained by her dedication to her art. She has that ease with the language that distinguishes the professional. But she has had less than professional training and so fewer of the usual professional's inhibitions. Beyond her dedication lies a quiet dignity that has kept her writing clear and unforced. She makes a tender subject, her family, of absorbing interest, more with joy and insight than with tricks and emotional pyrotechnics. Certainly what has happened to this normal, relatively well-off, moderate, untormented, respectable, settled family was neither soap opera nor late movie. The discussions and familiar activities of the family are recorded by the person who oversaw and orchestrated them in an old country house on graceful old grounds at gentle old Kennebunk Landing.

When you publish a newspaper in Maine the abundant crop of writers sees you as an outlet for authorly enthusiasms. To avoid inundation you must pick and choose carefully. Joyce Butler was an immediate choice, but not because her subject matter and gentle optimism fit the usual concept of journalism; they have more to do with the sort of relaxed uninterrupted reading you do after supper when the room is quiet than with the sort associated with the lunch counter and the coffee break. Among periodicals, only weekly newspapers and monthly magazines are normally read this way, the way Joyce Butler's work must be read. The light that shines through the words is pure and steadfast. A strong but unpretentious, optimistic but not pollyannic, force drives the quiet messages home.

The columns ramble from subject to subject, from review to report to account to essay, all held together with the thread of a quality of country life shaped by surroundings and seasons, maybe a bit old-fashioned, may very well be. Husband Bob still manages the family furniture business in Saco, and Joyce still caters to the family's needs and influences its life with perception, gentle wit and a strong sense of tradition. I have to guess that the columns themselves have played a role in the family melodrama and have had an influence on the family destiny, like Joyce herself actors as well as scribes in the same Kennebunk Landing life.

Alexander B. Brook
Publisher
York County Coast Star
Kennebunk, Maine
July 24, 1975

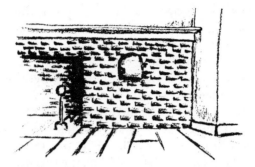

the house

We bought this house because it is old. People who want to own an old house cannot give too much consideration to its location or how many bedrooms it has or how much work will be involved in making it livable. People who love old houses look instead for fireplaces that work, wide board floors, small-paned windows, and low ceilings.

I remember the first time I came here. It was a raw March day. The house had not been lived in for over a year, and the cold and dampness that pervaded the rooms was more penetrating than the cold outside. Yet there was warmth here, a sense of waiting, of resignation to the bleak present state of things, and a feeling of "This too shall pass." Old houses are not quite inanimate. They live with Time. They endure. They have being!

A great deal of work needed to be done on the house, but on that cold, late-winter afternoon, as I walked through the rooms, I did not really see the peeling walls and ceilings. I was not aware that the dining room floor gave a little with each step. I didn't think about the furnace that sat in the middle of the kitchen floor. How could I, when there were sliding heat shutters in the windows, five fireplaces, a quaint "ship's stairway" rising out of the kitchen, wide pine boards on the floors, pine sheathing and a crooked little cupboard beside the fireplace in what I had already decided would be our "best parlor."

Later, when the house was ours, and we had begun the work of making it livable, a carpenter who had struggled all one day to plumb up a floor said to me, "My gosh, Missus! What do you folks see in these old houses?" I couldn't tell him. Those whose main concern is with plumb lines and efficiency find it difficult to value old houses.

From the beginning we were anxious to know the date of our house. Part of the adventure of owning it was to know when it was built and to try to fit it into the history of the town. The section of Kennebunk in which our house stands is called "The Landing." Years ago ships were built on the river that runs past our door, and the lumber to build them was brought by wagons and "landed" on the banking nearby. The bridge that crosses the river just below our house was once a draw bridge. It was opened when the ships were warped down to the mouth of the river where their masts were raised.

The last Indian raid to take place in this area occurred just down the river. A band of Indians set upon the homestead of a family named Durrell, while the men were away from home loading supplies on a ship at the mouth of the river, and carried off the women and children.

We wondered what connection our house had with this history, so I drove to Alfred, the county seat, to research our title. It was not difficult to discover that our house stands on a piece of land that was purchased in 1798 by "John Stone", of Arundel, Mariner." In 1803 he sold to "Israel Stone, of Arundel, Yeoman" the parcel "being the whole lot of land on which the said Stone now lives, *with the new dwelling house standing thereon,* and containing twelve acres."

I was elated. Here was not only a glimpse into that obsolete world of mariners and yeomen which stimulates the imagination and accounts in part for the attraction we feel for the old, but, more importantly, here was a direct reference to our house, placing its construction between 1798 and 1803. And yet, was this "new dwelling house" ours? We owned one acre of land. The twelve acres outlined in the deed would have included not only our land, but also property which had contained at least one, possibly two, other old houses. In the woods above us was an old cellar hole and below us toward the bridge was another house which was said to be built on the site of an older dwelling. Was our house the one in which Israel Stone had lived? It was highly probable, but was it legally certain? The distinction is an important one to students of history and old houses.

To be certain, I would have to research all of the deeds dealing with the area. This called for a surveyor's knowledge of lot lines and boundaries and would be a time consuming project. I lacked the skill, but a lack of time was the more important factor. It was the fall of the year; winter was coming and the old house had to be winterized. One step in this process was to take up the floor boards in the attic and lay insulation under them. We planned to do the work ourselves.

Work on old houses holds unexpected rewards. This tedious chore yielded special compensation. The cracks between the boards were wide and through them had fallen, over the years, stray fragments of the possessions of the inhabitants of the house. As each board was lifted we found intriguing treasure: the leather top of a high-button shoe, a heavily laden key ring, an 1825 Boston newspaper listing for sale the cargoes of recently arrived ships — St. Croix rum, bolts of Russia Duck, figs, opium, Otto of Rose, rye coffee, Corsica wine, and ermine robes. We found Victorian paperdolls, a fragment of a letter dated 1838, metal buttons, the porcelain arms of a small doll and one of her wooden legs, a tiny hand carved pig, half of a hair curling iron, and — happy discovery — one small, white card bearing the name "Israel Stone."

After that I thought of Israel often. Life in his house was strangely disquieting, not because he was here but because he was not. I met no ghosts on the steep back stairs at twilight. It would have seemed more fitting if I had. It bothered me that a man could build himself a house and live in it and then be gone and forgotten except for the kind of mischance that had brought Israel's existence to light. I found myself looking for the essence of him in the quaint structures of the house. Had he, Biblical Yankee, put the plain, plank mantle over the dining room fireplace because it was strong and serviceable though not elegant? Who could ever say?

And then one October day when the sunshine held the last strength of summer, I went looking for Israel in a different place. I went to an old cemetery nearby. The grey monuments canted over the old mounds. I read each one, but only in a far corner did I find "Elizabeth Stone, daughter of I. and P. Stone" and "Phebe Stone, wife of I. E. Stone" and finally on a fallen marker, embedded in moss, its lettering almost worn away:

ISRAEL STONE
Died
Mar. 15, 1857
A.E. 81
The memory of the just is blessed.

I had been seeking proof of the man, more than could be found in dusty legal records or even in a still vital house. I had my proof.

I still think of Israel, but only occasionally, and there is comfort in knowing that I am living in his house.

the cats

It has been a year now since our black cat came to us. That sounds very fine, but it was not so fine a thing as I remember it. It was simply a case of a stray cat who would not take no for an answer. She followed us home from a walk one snowy afternoon, enchanting the children with her sidewise caperings down the road and her leg-rubbing entreaties to be noticed. Bob and I took great care not to notice her, knowing that it is easy for a cat lover to love any cat; almost easier than it is for a stray cat to attach itself to a family.

When we reached home and shut the door upon her she hunkered down on the narrow doorstep, a ball of black against the yellow door.

"She wants to come in," observed Jamie.

"Can't we let her in?" asked Leslie.

"She is *not* coming in," said Bob. "We've got enough cats."

"She's probably hungry. Can't we take a bowl of milk out to her?" Stephanie suggested.

"No, no, we musn't feed her," I explained. "Once you've fed a cat he's yours."

As the afternoon wore on the children went now and then to the window.

"She's still there," reported Leslie.

"Poor kitty," mourned Stephanie. Bob shook his head. To myself I said, "Poor kitty." At last the sun went down. The cold became more intense and still the cat hugged the yellow door. The children didn't leave the window now.

"She must be cold," said Leslie.

"Look, she's crying," cried Stephanie. Bob and I went to look. The black cat was crying to the row of faces in the window, showing her sharp, white teeth.

"Poor kitty," I said softly.

"She wants something to eat," said Leslie.

"Then feed her!" Bob exclaimed.

"Hurrah," cried the children rushing to the door. I hurried to the refrigerator. Once inside the house the black cat immediately nose-dived into the wastebasket in search of food. We fed her and the pact was sealed.

The children were delighted. Bob and I felt resignation. But poor Adam and Eve — their attitude toward this new member of our household was entirely different. Adam and Eve are our *other* cats.

Adam and Eve have lived with us since they were kittens. They are brother and sister. In the beginning we named them "Kit" and "Kat," but because it seemed that we spoke most often of them as "the boy cat" and "the girl cat" we re-named them "Adam" and "Eve." There is irony here, for a trip to the veterinarian had made it certain that neither would propagate their species.

Adam and Eve were aghast at the presence of the black kitten in our household. In the beginning they were afraid of her and would not eat beside her, but ran to hide upstairs. This gave rise to our choice of name for her. We call her "Hero"! The name was an honorific, in a sense, but mostly we were conveying our disgust with Adam and Eve who wouldn't stand their ground. It was irritating to have to deal with the nonsense of the two older, larger cats. It was a nuisance to have to feed them at a separate time or in a different room or else to have to rescue their abandoned food from Hero who would, we discovered, gladly eat three bowls of cat food per meal.

Poor Adam and Eve. I believe they suffered a little. It is difficult when middle-aged, complacent, and set in one's ways to have a youngster appear on the scene to disrupt one's life. And Hero recognized the advantage they gave her and made the most of it.

Adam, at that time, was recovering from a vitamin deficiency that had caused all the hair to fall off the back of his hind legs. He was a sorry sight to see — in retreat; rather like a skinny old man in his nightshirt. The children and I talked of making him some polka-dotted bloomers to cover his nakedness! Unfortunately, Hero was quick to see an advantage there and took to nipping him on his hindquarters, darting in upon him when he was least prepared; for example, when he was stretching after a cozy nap. Poor Adam!

For Eve, Hero devised a different harassment. Eve is fat and quite a proper lady as only the overweight female can be. She minces a little when she walks and runs like a distracted hen. Eve is something of a ninny-noddy. And oh, the mortification she suffered, for Hero would lie in wait for her, behind the couch or around a corner, and pounce out upon her in great glee to send her rolling, and meowing, and at last running.

We did much placating in those early days, and wondered what the outcome of Hero's campaign would be, for a campaign it had become. It was apparent that our black interloper had decided to clear the field and claim her new found comfort exclusively for herself.

But Adam and Eve had roots here and they also come from good barn stock. They cannot claim breeding, but they have had upbringing. The day came when Adam had had enough and his long dormant masculinity asserted itself. Eunuch he might be, but within him beats the heart of a Tom. Hero nipped once too often, and Adam turned on her and sent her rolling. Hero accepted the challenge and turned with youthful zest to fight. But Adam stood his ground. He was magnificent to see! He planted his front paws firmly in a noble stance, lowered his great broad head and held it steady, fixed his eyes in a menacing stare on some spot just over the black cat's head, fluffed his tail and waved it rhythmically. And then he talked! Such meowings and yowlings I had heard before only on back yard fences. I could easily imagine what he said. Surely he claimed franchise and surely there were threats too in case the former argument carried no weight with the young, black whippersnapper.

Hero heard, and she mended her ways. I must admit capitulation did not come immediately. Adam had more than one session with that cat, but at last Hero got the point, for she quietly took her place in the ranks and seemed content to do so.

Eve reaped the benefit of Adam's determination, but I must say a word for her too. Ninny-noddy she may be, but she has a mind of her own. It is to her credit that one day I found her, frustrated mother that she is, planted squarely on top of Hero giving her a bath.

the beach

I went to the beach today, not to swim or sit on the sand, but to fill my lungs with fresh air and to stretch my legs walking the winter strand. I saw no other walkers: not many people venture to the shore of the sea when its shingle is coated with ice.

I left the car on the road and climbed over the seawall. I stood a minute in the yellow tangle of the beach grass that grows between the wall and the beach, and looked out to sea. Far to the left purple hills looked like cutouts against the winter-white sky. On the horizon where the sky met the ocean, the water was slate grey and looked flat. Nearer to shore it was blue-green and opaque and moved in choppy little waves. Closer still to shore, where it curled into gentle breakers, the water was pale green and lipped with foam, and the sliding waves, running onto the shore, were spread with foam that looked like lace laid on heavy, green satin.

The beach was strewn with kelp, rocks, and debris that storms had brought up on the sand. The kelp, dark green and black, was piled in mounds at the water's edge. It smelled of salt, a wild, natural scent that made me think of the depths of the ocean and the elements having their way with seaweed and stones.

There were stones on the beach — flat, smooth, grey. They lay in a ragged swath up the curve of the shore, and against them the waves had broken the shells of mussels, clams, periwinkles and other mollusks which come out of the sea in this part of the world. Seagulls break shells open on rocks too. Looking up the beach I saw a gull swoop low and drop a mussel from his beak. He followed it down to pick the meat out of the broken shell.

Besides the kelp, the stones, and the broken shells there was wood on the beach. I gathered it from the cold sand. Much of it was still dense, good for the fire, and would, I knew, burn with color and fill the room with the smell and taste of salt. Nails, rusty now and twined with kelp, pierced it, and knotholes stared from it like angry eyes. I wondered whose wharf had fallen into the sea.

There were pieces of lobster trap to be salvaged too, latticework to lay on the fire. An occasional piece of driftwood, bleached white as bone by the salt water, ribbed, contorted, reduced during its time in the sea to a skeleton of its former self, was too beautiful for burning. Such pieces I saved for display on the mantle or a wide window sill. I wondered if this wood came from the rotting hull of a dory beached somewhere on the shore of the nearby tidal river.

I carried the driftwood to the car, making more than one trip back and forth, scavenging each time further up the shore until I came almost to the point of land where the summer hotel sits; shuttered, waiting, no red geraniums and trailing ivy in its window boxes, no bright gathering of umbrellas on its lawn. And that was when I realized how cold I was. My cheeks tingled, and the tips of my fingers were icy inside my mittens. I turned and hurried back along the shore, eager to get home for a warming cup of tea.

the mice

I think the mice have moved out. I haven't heard them lately. They must have noticed how blue the sky is these days and how butter-yellow the sun that splashes through the dining room windows. Not that they were in the dining room! They have lived under the attic floor boards and inside the walls. But the heat of the sun on the roof and walls of the house must have communicated itself to them. I hope so. Stephanie and I had begun to dispair for them because Bob was talking ominously about "doing something about those mice."

They moved in last fall, coming in, I suppose, from the fields. We knew they had come because their exploring around the center chimney attracted the attention of the cats who would sit in the chimney corner staring fixedly at the woodwork near the fireplace. Noticing the cats we would be still, and then we'd hear the gentle scratching behind the wainscot. But the cats couldn't get to them, and eventually the mice stopped exploring down inside the house. And so we forgot them.

I was reminded of their presence after Christmas when I went into the attic to put the tree ornaments away. I discovered that the swag of wheat and dried things I hang on the front door from September to December had been dined upon. After that, for a week or two, we put one of the cats in the attic at night. Each morning the cat would emerge from behind the closed door looking rested, acting self-satisfied, and feeling very hungry. We didn't know whether the mice had been caught, but we stopped putting a cat in the attic.

I didn't think of the mice again until one evening in early March. I was sitting on Stephanie's bed waiting for her to brush her teeth so I could tuck her in for the night. Sitting in the quiet room, glad to be still a minute after another busy day, I heard, suddenly, a scrabbling and scratching in the ceiling and then a crunching-gnawing sort of noise.

"Stephanie," I called. "Listen!" She came in from the bathroom and stood in the doorway listening.

"Oh, yes," she said. "The mice."

"Ah," I said, remembering. "The mice. They've gotten into your ceiling."

"I hear them every night," Stephanie told me. "There's a quiet one and a noisy one." She listened a minute to the crunching-gnawing sound. "That's the noisy one. I've named him Tom Thumb. The other one's Hunca Munca—you know, after the mice in the book who get into the doll house and carry things away." I knew she was referring to Beatrix Potter's *Tale of Two Bad Mice.* "I make believe they come out of the ceiling and take things out of my doll house and carry them up to the house Tom Thumb is building in my ceiling. It's got lots of rooms and passageways."

I listened to Tom Thumb's noisy work with mixed feelings, visualizing a little parlor furnished with stools and pictures and curtains spirited away from the doll house, while at the same time thinking about real mice with sharp teeth gnawing at the beams in our house. I thought about Stephanie lying between sleeping and waking, making up stories in her mind about the mice, her imaginings slipping into dreams to carry her through the night.

"Well, Stephanie," I said, "I at least hope they don't have babies." But Stephanie would not let me be comforted.

"Oh, but in the book they have babies, Mama. Lots of them!"

I hadn't remembered that part of the story, so after tucking her in I carried the little book downstairs and re-read it and looked at the charming pictures. I found myself picturing Stephanie's mice with pink shell ears, bright beady eyes, and luxurious whiskers. I visualized the quiet mouse wearing a gown of sprigged muslin and a cambric apron. After that it was difficult for me to think about curtailing the laborings of Tom Thumb.

It was about a week later that the mice moved into the downstairs woodwork again. They came in the evening when Bob was sitting on the couch reading. Unfortunately it was Tom Thumb, the noisy mouse, who came, and he was very noisy. Eve the Cat rose up from a sound sleep to track his movements inside the wall, and Bob scowled and said, "Those mice are back."

The next morning at breakfast he said, "I've got to do something about those mice."

"Not Hunca Munca," cried Stephanie. "Not Tom Thumb!"

"Who? What?" said her father.

"You see, Daddy," Stephanie explained, "I've named the mice after the mice in a book, and I pretend that Tom Thumb is building a house in my ceiling . . ."

"Yes, that's probably just what he's doing," said Bob grimly.

Stephanie could see she'd made the wrong point so she went on, "But Daddy, they're going to have babies!"

"Exactly!" Poor Stephanie. She was learning that the fiction we read is not always transferable to the fact of real life.

Bob never did do anything about the mice and now that spring is really here I think they have left the house for their summer home in the field. I hope so, and I hope also that Stephanie's Hunca Munca is a good mother like Beatrix Potter's and has been very sure that she has taken ALL of her babies with her.

mothers

"It seems to me that in books the kids who have all the fun don't have a mother," said eleven-year-old Leslie. The remark startled me because quick reflection made me realize that it was a true statement. Take Nancy Drew for example. She's the girl who has all the marvelous adventures with haunted houses and evil people. And look at Tom Sawyer and Huck Finn and Heidi. Not a one had a mother and they had wonderful adventures. While it is true that they suffered also, everything came out all right in the end, didn't it? There is no doubt about it: from the point of view of an eleven-year-old with an independent spirit, having a mother can be a very serious handicap.

Besides wanting to know where a girl is all the time mothers are negative about lots of things that are important . . . like Go-Go Boots and the latest hair styles (mothers are always saying, "Push your hair back so I can see your pretty, young face."). Mothers insist on an 8:30 bedtime on school nights even though "All the other kids stay up till eleven." And mothers are fussy about what television programs you watch, ruling out "Dark Shadows" and the science fiction movie on Friday. And mothers are so *positive* (and persistent) about things like piano lessons and keeping your room picked up and having a shampoo. Mothers are old as well as being old fashioned and it seems that life would be much easier if only you didn't have a mother to contend with.

Of course there are times when having a mother is a comfort.

Sometimes you have a fight with your best friend and you come home upset and cross and instead of saying, "We don't need any grouches around here" your mother says, "What's the matter? Can I help?" and in a burst of gratitude you tell her what happened. She listens and then nods her head and says quietly, "Something like that happened to me once." You look at her in surprise and say, "It did?" She tells you all about it and, because talking about your mother's experience makes you see what happened between you and your friend and makes you realize that things will be all right between you again, you feel a great sense of relief. It's wonderful when this happens and a girl feels lighthearted and can't wait to get back to school the next day to see her best friend, and everything is fine until supper when Mother says, "Eat your peas." Then, because you resent being treated like a child, you snap, "I'm *going* to" and feel cross.

Mothers have their daily virtues too, of course. When you come home from school you rush into the house and throw your books on the kitchen table and holler, "Hi, Mum, I'm home." And it isn't really enough to hear her voice call from some distant room, "Hi, dear." You have to go find her, and you tell her all about your day as fast as you can in competition with brothers and sisters who have a lot to tell too. And then you ask, "What's for a snack?" Sometimes you don't have to ask because when you come through the door the warm smell of spicy cookies greets you. Sometimes the cookies are shaped like leaves (in the fall) or hearts (in February) or rabbits (at Easter time). Mothers make homemade bread too.

And mothers have other virtues. When you are eleven you can take for granted having clean and freshly ironed clothes in your closet all the time. And you offer to bring cookies for a party at school because you know your mother will make them. And at Girl Scouts when they need extra cars to go on a field trip you say, "My mother will drive" because you know she will.

Besides being convenient mothers can be fun. Like on May Day when you are finishing your supper and Mother excuses herself from the table and the next thing you know there's a loud knock at the door. You go and there is a *huge* May basket and you run around the corner of the house to see who left it and there's Mother hiding behind the lilac bush. She runs and you chase her and she looks so funny leaping through the tall grass in the field. Finally your little brother catches her and you all are breathless from running and laughing.

But the trouble with mothers is that even when they are being good they are a problem. Mothers are so . . . *maternal:* always wanting to pat you or call you "dear" or just to *look* at you. Somehow having a mother doesn't really go with being an adult, which is what you want to be more than anything else when you are eleven years old. And then there are the times when mothers don't understand and are unfair or too strict. As Leslie's mother I understand that this happens better than she does.

I appreciate the burden I am to Leslie, but I'm afraid she's just going to have to suffer through (and so am I). And things are not going to get easier right away. We still have to face the hurdles of lipstick, nylons, and boy friends. But there are good times ahead of us too. As she grows I'll share with her what I know of the mysteries of cooking and make-up and men; and, if I'm lucky and have kept our lines of communication open, she'll share with me the fun she has at pajama parties, exchange concerts, and dances, and her youthful views will keep me in touch with the times.

Then she'll be free of home and will go on to more school or a job or marriage and having won her independence she'll savor it. But I think when she comes home to visit and finds the same spicy cookies in the cookie jar and sees in my face that terrible familiarity that I see in the aging face of *my* mother . . . then she'll be glad she has a mother, and the reason why won't be easily discernable, but will be all bound up in what Leslie has learned about herself and people and life, and with a nostalgic appreciation for that part of her life that is gone into memory.

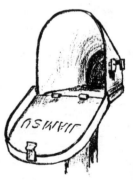

grammy b.

She died in the spring, our Grammy B. People say we did not have any spring that year. The cold and snow hung on well into April. I remember that on the day we buried her snow fell in big, flat, wet flakes that made a heavy slush on the ground. I wonder how we could have stood her slow dying if it had been otherwise. If the new green had begun in the fields, if the buds on the trees had been soft and yielding, how could we have lived with the fact of her dying? And how could we have looked again to spring?

When a distant relative dies, or a sometime neighbor, or

someone whose story we have heard from mutual friends, we give lip service to his passing. We say, "I'm so sorry" or "It's a blessing." It isn't that our expressions of sympathy are not sincere; it's just that we stand on the fringes of the event: our feelings have not been touched. But then comes the death of someone whose life was meshed with our own, someone who had dimension for us as a human being. This was a person who shared with us his thoughts. We saw his zest for living. We watched his work. We understood his prejudices. We knew of his ambitions. And this is when we begin to understand about dying.

Perhaps this person once said to us, "I don't think I'll ever be ready to die. There's too much I want to learn and so much I want to do and so many things are going to happen in this world that I want to know about." Remembering this we understand that we have been spectators at a kind of performance whose final outcome was always beyond control. With this awareness of what was lost to him comes also the realization of what is lost to each of us ... even as we are born, even as we are young and healthy and important. As we have spoken glibly of "when I die" so now, when we have seen the passing of a strong, vital, grasping force that was a human being, we comprehend that indeed we shall die. And then we are afraid, and our fear of the inflexible course we are pursuing is part of our grief.

Grief leads back to self not just because of fear, but also because we have lost someone who cared about us and in caring enriched our life. If the business of living clouds the structure of human relationships, death throws it all into sharp relief. Stark is the telephone that does not bring the daily hello, large is the loss of the weekly letter, lonely are the mealtimes, filled with gaps are the holiday celebrations.

Grief is for the living because it has little meaning for the dead. When someone we have valued dies even those of us without religious convictions sense that for him this is a positive achievement. We find it possible to believe that "death is not the worst thing that can happen; only the last."*

We grieve for what is gone, but we ask too what is left. It is surprising how much. What a human being has given of himself to others in kindness, encouragement, cheer, remains and gives meaning to the fact that he lived. Those of us who lived close to him discover that he has also left us a legacy of attitudes, tradition, example, and the measure of wisdom which comes out of the experience of losing him. And perhaps that is where the healing

*Philip Wylie, *The Innocent Ambassadors,* Rinehart, 1957

begins. We become for a time a little more gentle and wise, and we grow a step or two into maturity. And some of us, having asked ourselves what part of his life was important, are able to make of our questioning an equation to the meaning and importance of the life we ourselves are living. Then for us the gauntlet is down and this too is part of the legacy.

the gardens

It began a month ago. The gardens which surround our house overcame once more their frost-pocked crusts, and green living things began to show themselves amid the brown disarray of last year's growth. The weeds came first, popping full grown and lusty from the soil, but some of the flowers followed close behind, putting forth their first tentative shoots while the roots of other plants waited below the ground for their time to grow. And so it has begun again: the progression of bloom that paces us through the spring and summer months.

The gardens were here before us. We did not plant them, and in the beginning did not value them, but viewed them with some alarm, being non-gardeners. It was the house we wanted, but the gardens went with the house, living appendages, as it were.

Mrs. Lyons, the lady who had lived here before us, planted the gardens. We never knew her, but neighbors told us that she had loved flowers the way some people love children. Certainly she must have loved the work of growing them; the fifteen or more flower beds she made here were proof of that.

Because my ignorance about gardening was complete, one or two gardens would have been a challenge to me. I didn't comprehend the magnitude of the task before me when I set out to reclaim *all* the gardens. And a reclamation project it was, for they were long neglected. Mrs. Lyons had grown old here and her age and illness, plus the difficulty of hiring other hands, had left the gardens to nature's selection. They had become weed and grass and moss infested.

Through our first winter here I waited impatiently for the spring. When the snow was gone and the drying winds had swept through the yard I began the work of reclaiming the garden near the back door. As I worked there all my senses, dulled by the years spent in classrooms, in apartment-house-living, in making a home and filling it with children, came alive again. I smelled the almost offensive odor of fecund springtime dirt. I felt the sun hot upon my shoulders, and was aware of the call of a phoebe bird floating down from high in a pine tree at the back of the yard. And when the flowers came, tentatively at first — Johnny-jump-ups with their miniature pansy faces, the white violets whose prolificacy caught me unprepared, the fragrant lilies of the valley — I saw them clearly as children do who spend long hours out-of-doors.

After the brave forerunners the other flowers came all in a rush sending me distracted from garden to garden in a vain attempt to keep order and to appreciate their variety. Naming them was a challenge in itself. I pored over gardening books and came to watch for particular flowers. Great was my delight when they appeared. Friends who came to visit were all subjected to a tour of the gardens in the hope that they could name a plant, and invariably each visitor could name at least one.

Each day I visited each garden to see what new flowers had appeared. I came out early in the morning while the grass was still wet. I made my rounds in the afternoon and again at night before the last light faded. In the long twin gardens beyond the house I watched the columbine begin as tightly curled, maroon leaves — cups to hold early morning dew — fanning soon and turning to green to complement the blossoms of dull blue, or rich purple, or double white, or pale pink, or a striking variety of bright purple and white together.

One plant I had watched putting forth fat buds bloomed one morning with large yellow buttercups. This I learned to call a globeflower. Near it blossomed low clumps of blue Jacob's ladder and tall, blue spikes of Veronica and feathery puffs of white astilbe. Here too grew the Siberian iris: tall and short, dark blue and light blue.

The bearded iris grew in a garden near the driveway, tall beauties of pale yellow, dark brown, and white with blue beards. On the hill near the rose bushes and the old sweet pea garden I found another variety of iris, a rich deep yellow flower. And still there were the Japanese iris of white or lavender.

Peonies, white, pink and deep red, grew in a double row on the edge of the yard, their heavy blossoms leaning down to touch the masses of Star of Bethlehem that crowded about their stalks. Day lilies grew everywhere, at least six different varieties, and there were other lilies : white madonna, orange tiger, and a salmon colored variety that I still cannot name.

The evening primrose had run wild, as had the silver basket, the ground phlox, and pinks. Meadow rue and mallow, wild flowers, grew in the gardens, and at the back of the yard, minute violets and forget-me-not ran rampant in the grass. They had been planted on the edges of a small pond where Mrs. Lyons had kept goldfish and pond lilies and where a Blue Heron had come one evening to hunt the fish. The pond has long since dried away, and the story of the heron came to us from neighbors.

Yarrow, delphinium, everlasting, achilla, balloonflower, phlox, fox-glove, asters, beebalm, one lone plant of monkshood, a few straying bellflowers — all these appeared. Amid the profusion of these growing things I discovered herbs too: apple mint, spearmint, chives, thyme, and tarragon. The mint had spread to the grass so that when we mowed its fresh scent hung on the evening air.

It was exciting to discover the treasure we had acquired along with our rather special house, and as I learned to name each flower so too I learned to be a gardener. I learned the uses of bone meal and peat moss. I learned to water the gardens deeply so that roots would reach down into the ground and not lie near the surface. I discovered that weeding is easier after a rainfall. I learned about "rotation of bloom" and "juxtaposition of color and texture." I learned about aphids and spider mites, and about "pinching back," dormant periods, seed pods, rhizomes, and tap roots. But I discovered too how restful is an hour spent weeding the garden: good therapy for jangled nerves and a tired mind. I exchanged plants with fellow gardeners, and discovered the pleasure of being reminded of the friend when his gift plant blooms anew. And I learned the satisfaction that comes from creating beauty—for itself.

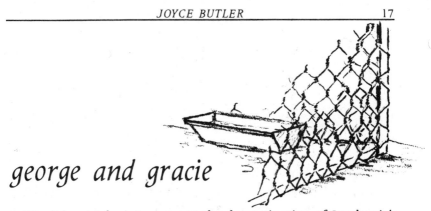

george and gracie

We did not take into account the determination of Stephanie's teacher to give her students a complete and meaningful educational experience. When Stephanie came home from school and told us about the incubator the teacher had set up in the classroom and asked if we would give permission for her to bring home a chick when the eggs hatched, we gave our permission. We knew something about the delicacy of hatching eggs in an incubator and felt fairly certain that most of the eggs would not hatch, meaning there would not be baby chickens for the children to take home.

We were right; most of the eggs did not hatch, but the teacher, not wanting the experiment to end on a negative note, drove miles to a chicken farm to collect a host of healthy baby chicks for the eager students. Thus it was that there was, after all, a chicken for Stephanie to bring home. In fact, on the day she went off to school with a box, lined with hay, in which to carry home her chick, she telephoned from school to ask if please could she bring home a baby hen *and* a baby rooster.

"You know, Mama," she said seriously. "The hen can't have babies without the rooster." The fact that Bob and I did not *want* the hen to have babies seemed irrelevant and thus it was that two black chicks came home to swell our menagerie of three cats, one goldfish, and a jar of pollywogs.

If the enthusiasm we adults showed for the newcomers was strained, the children didn't notice. Bob and I secretly harbored the thought that baby chicks are not too strong and this fact, coupled with our dangerous ignorance about raising chickens, gave us reason to believe that they probably would not survive.

We were wrong. They waxed strong and noisy on their diet of chick starter feed and in the glow of their pseudo-mother, a gooseneck lamp. I was impressed with the dedication of the children to caring for the chickens, and I appeased my feelings further by ordering the tadpoles back to the pond. The goldfish also cooperated by quietly dying, which was just as well in view of the fact that he had outlived his novelty and interest to us all.

When it became apparent that inner infirmity was not present in our chicks and when the children had named them George and Gracie, it was finally clear that here were pets to be reckoned with. It was at that point that I began to give serious consideration to the cats.

Eve was the first of the three to discover the chickens. She couldn't believe her ears when she heard them peeping or her eyes when she jumped up onto the washing machine and looked into their box. After that we never left the house without putting the box on top of the refrigerator, which seemed the only spot inaccessible to the climbing, jumping prowess of cats. I was a bit disconcerted to discover that *I* was as concerned about this precautionary measure as the children.

The next step was the loan, by a neighbor, of a wonderfully useful cage with three doors which gave us easy access to the feed and water dishes and to the chickens themselves. This was when the ritual of their daily run in the yard began. When we wanted to clean the cage we let George and Gracie loose upon the grass. Their joy at this treat was obvious. Indeed, as they grew older they set up a great clatter when any of us approached the cage, thinking it was time for their daily stroll in the garden. Eventually as they grew larger, lifting them through the small doors became a ticklish matter, and we discovered that if we opened one of the doors they would come out on their own.

Once freedom was gained they would fly up off the ground with a great flapping of their wings, squawking their pleasure at this opportunity for exercise. They also liked to roll in the dirt. Eventually we learned that this was normal procedure for chickens, but in the beginning it was new to us, and I must admit entertaining.

George and Gracie grew and grew. George began to develop his red wattles and comb, and we could detect sounds of an incipient crow rumbling around in his throat. On one happy day they were taken back to school to display their fine selves to the class, and I don't know whose pleasure was greater—that of the class or that of the Butlers who proudly paraded the cage into the room. I guess it was on that day that I finally admitted to myself that I had become attached to George and Gracie.

The question of the survival of the chickens still hung over us. It was obvious that they had just about outgrown their cage and it was time to put them into an outdoor pen. Bob made them a fenced yard on the hill behind a screening arbor of climbing bittersweet. It was a good size pen with high walls of chicken wire. George and Gracie could at last enjoy unlimited scratching and rolling in the dirt. Bob and I wondered vaguely about tunneling animals, and climbing animals, and chicken hawks, but shrugged and said resignedly to each other, "What will be will be."

On the morning after George and Gracie's first night in their new pen, Stephanie was up and dressed and down to breakfast earlier than usual. She breezed through the kitchen, announcing as she went, "I'm going to see how George and Gracie liked their first night in the new pen." It seemed that she had only been gone a minute before we heard her running steps. She burst into the kitchen calling, "They're gone. They're gone. George and Gracie are gone."

Ah! It had happened. Bob and I exchanged glances. We had been afraid it would come, but not so soon. It didn't seem fair for it to have come so soon. Poor George and Gracie. Frying bacon, perking coffee and the morning news report forgotten, we followed Stephanie up the hill, the other children, half dressed for school, running close behind. We stood in the wet grass staring into the empty pen. And it was *so* empty. There was not a sign of a feather. There was no evidence of a struggle. There was no hole in the fence and no tunnel under it. Bob and I were puzzled. It seemed unlikely that a marauding animal would not leave some sign of his presence and his destructive errand. As we stood in silence, puzzling over the mystery, we heard behind us a faint rustling noise. Turning and looking up into the arbor of bittersweet we saw George and Gracie roosting together on the sturdy vine.

"George! Gracie! You're all right. Oh, I'm so glad, Mama. I was so afraid. Aren't you glad, Mama?" Yes, I was glad.

After that it was all pleasure. George and Gracie spent their days in sunny, dirt-scratching comfort, but once dusk arrived they would fly up into the bittersweet vine to roost for the night. Dawn found them ready for breakfast, and they walked down the hill to the back door where they pecked at the screen as if to say, "Come on, get up. We're hungry." When one of us appeared at the door with the bag of feed, off they would run up the hill to their pen for breakfast and another docile day.

I took to checking them each evening. After touring the gardens to see how the flowers grew, I would go up the hill to see if the chickens had gone to roost. Invariably Gracie would have settled herself for the night. Often George was still on the ground enjoying a last scratch and search for worms. I would lift him up into the vine and he would clumsily work his way over to Gracie, for they always roosted side by side, snuggling in for all the world like old married folk. In the morning we laughed to find them at the back door, watched from afar by the three equally hungry cats who were afraid of the chickens and had thus allowed their breakfast vigil to be moved out to the edge of the yard.

But one morning George and Gracie did not appear at the door. I kept going to the window to look for them, thinking perhaps they had slept late or were breakfasting on worms as they came. But, at last, when they still did not appear and thinking again of animals who like to eat young chicken, I did not wait for the children to get downstairs to carry feed to the pen. I went myself. Thus it was that I was the one to find the pitiful little pile of black chicken feathers on the edge of the garden among the broken stalks of flowers and near the paw marks of a racoon. We don't know what happened beyond the fact that it was a racoon who took George and Gracie, but we suspect that their demise came as they sauntered down to the back door in search of breakfast.

Silly old chickens. I regret your empty pen. I regret your small tragedy. I'm glad we had the pleasure of you and only wish it had not been so brief.

jamie

He is six and a half years old, and watching him I realize that my tree climbing days are over. There was a time, a year or so ago, when I was called on quite often to scale tall trees to retrieve a frightened little boy whose adventuresome spirit led him to climb higher than the extent of his courage. But now that he is six and a half he wouldn't dream of calling on his mother in such a situation. And besides, these days his courage knows no bounds.

Jamie, or Jim Butler as Bob calls him, has made great strides during the last few months. For example, he can whistle now. Learning to whistle was very important to Jamie and there were moments when he wondered out loud and with despair if he'd ever master the skill. But perseverance, a few vague pointers from startled adults who had never given the mechanics of whistling much thought, and practice sessions at bedtime in the privacy of his dark room have brought results. Jamie can whistle ... breathless little bird-call melodies.

Since whistling is his newest accomplishment Jamie offers it as his contribution when company comes. Leslie and Stephanie exhibit new skills with the clarinet or relate progress in swimming, but Jamie sits near the visitor and whistles and waits to be noticed. If his new skill is commented upon he will also snap his fingers and this display of achievement in tandem with the whistling seldom fails to impress. If, however, the visitor does not take note of the performance, Jamie accepts this as part of life and goes outside to renew his faith in himself with a few daring turns around the driveway on his two-wheeler.

Jamie has made other gains too. He has lost his two front teeth and is growing new ones which seem too big and square for his mouth. The first front tooth came out during an overnight visit at a friend's house. An inadvertant swipe with a baseball bat knocked it out and that night it was put under his pillow in the unfamiliar bed in hopes that the Blue Fairy would come. She did. Our whole family was impressed when we heard, for in this household the Blue Fairy is very forgetful and a tooth sometimes stays under a pillow for two nights before it is replaced with a dime.

Yes, Jamie is growing up. We watch him grow without regret even though he is the "baby" of the family and even though we realize that as he marks milestones in his development, milestones are also being struck off for us. Perhaps we do not begrudge his progress because we are too busy enjoying it.

Jamie gives joy as he goes. He always has. Across the short span of his years he has exhibited a collection of happy mannerisms and has entertained us with his comments on and dealings with life. When he was four he would tug at a sleeve to be noticed and say, "I want to tell you something." When we leaned down to listen he would say, "I like you." When he was five his two greatest pleasures were being with his father and working: pounding nails, scraping floor boards, pushing a lawn mower, shoveling snow. One Sunday he had dogged Bob's footsteps all day giving freely of his energy to various projects, maintaining a constant stream of chatter and questions, prefacing each remark with "Daddy." "Daddy, what are we going to do now?"

"Daddy, we're doing a good job, aren't we!"

"Daddy, when are we going to mow the lawn?"

"Daddy, why are you doing that?" Finally, Bob in exasperation, born of fatigue, said, "Jim, I'll give you a nickel for every time you don't say 'Daddy'." Jamie lapsed into silence, thinking, and then said, "Mr. Butler, I want to use that saw." A nickel went into his bank that night.

We watch Jamie grow, catching his witticisms as they come, harboring (if truth be told) the feeling that he is rather special. But one of the nicest things about him is that he is just a six year old who is growing up. Parents everywhere stand before their offspring enjoying their entertaining ways and clever remarks and preserving them as family history. Jamie is not unique; he is just ours.

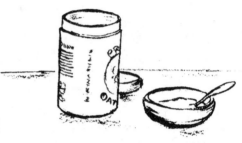

jessie brown

My day began with sunlight and birdsong and that was not unusual. I went about my work filled with that sense of well-being that comes from an unconscious acceptance of daily abundance and security.

The phone rang early. It was Ruth Goode, and she was calling to talk to me about Jessie Brown. Jessie Brown lives in Mississippi. She is black. She is also poor, and she has six children. Ruth and her husband, who have five children of their own, had been put in touch with Jessie through an organization that tries to find families who will help needy people in the South by sending them boxes of food and used clothing. I had heard about Ruth's commitment to Jessie Brown at a church meeting and had promised to do what I could to find used clothing and to buy, now and then, supplies of dried milk, raisins, oatmeal and other nourishing food.

After mailing a box of food at Easter time, Ruth had called and said, "It cost me $2.00 to send that last box. Doesn't it seem too bad to spend that money on postage when it could go for more food. I wonder if Mrs. Brown is eligible for federal food stamps, and if she is, do you suppose we could help her get started on the program? Probably her welfare payments are so small that she can't get enough money ahead to be able to buy a month's supply of stamps, but if we could send her enough money to get her on the program maybe she could save enough out of her welfare check to buy the next supply of stamps." We agreed that Ruth should look into the matter and call me when she knew more about it. And now she was calling.

"I've heard from Mrs. Brown," said Ruth. "I knew her welfare payments were small, but I was really shocked to find out that she only gets $51.00 a month. She pays $15.00 a month rent (for that price they must live in a real shack), and $6.00 a month for electricity. She didn't mention heat so they must have a wood stove. She said she'd like to get food stamps but if she signed up just for the children it would cost $52.00 a month. That means that even if we sent her the money for a month's supply of stamps she wouldn't be able to keep it up."

"Well, what shall we do?" I asked. "Are you still going to try to get her on the program for June?"

"Yes, I'd like to. That would be one month's meals anyway. And maybe we could find some other family to go in on this with us. If we could send her part of the money each month, that would be something. But isn't it shocking and discouraging that these people are so poor they can't even afford to take advantage of charity! No wonder she's been so grateful for the boxes we've sent. But what hope does she have!"

Jessie Brown was in my thoughts all day. When I hung out the washing, birds sang in the trees overhead, and I wondered if Jessie Brown heard birdsong or if her listening ear was turned inward to a persistent voice that questioned, "What'm I goin' to give those kids for supper?"

And my thinking went beyond Jessie to the larger questions of welfare, and ran the gamut of arguments pro and con:

"Welfare becomes a way of life. You can find generations in one family who are willing to live on a dole." (But who would really prefer welfare if he had a choice between it and self-sufficiency?)

"If all the money in the world were divided up equally tomorrow among all the people in the world, next year there would be people living in poverty." (Yes, but haven't we got to try to help the poor for the sake of those who *would* do better?)

"You go to church and call yourself a Christian: how come you don't give away all your worldly goods like it says in the Bible?" (I'm not that good a Christian, I guess.)

"Why are we spending billions on a space program instead of helping the poor?" (Because man needs new horizons; he needs a dream.)

But what is Jessie Brown's dream? Her dream is for oatmeal for breakfast and curtains at the window. ("Oh, Mrs. Goode, thank you for the oatmeal. The children liked it for breakfast. Could you send some more? And, oh Mrs. Goode, could you send me some curtains?")

My thinking comes back again and again to Jessie Brown and her six children. Beyond the knowledge that thousands of welfare dollars are spent each year I am faced with the fact of Jessie Brown's family . . . still hungry, still in need of the bare necessities of life. The words of a song that the children learned in Sunday School run through my mind:

Up, up, with people!
You meet 'em wherever you go.
Up, up, with people!
They're the best kind of folks we know.
If more people were for people,
All people everywhere,
There'd be a lot less people to worry about
And a lot more people who care.*

People caring about people. Isn't that an answer? In the face of the seemingly insurmountable problem of the poor isn't aid to one *known* needy family a beginning? What was it Eleanor Roosevelt said: "I'd rather light one candle than curse the darkness."

How many people would it take to help Jessie Brown, just to give her food on her table and perhaps a little hope? It would take twelve families who would give one dollar a week. If twelve families gave one dollar a week Jessie Brown could buy one month's supply of food stamps. And what would those twelve families be sacrificing: a carton of Coca Cola this week, one less flat of seedlings for the garden last week, the absence of daisy decals on the station wagon this summer. And from such sacrifices Jessie Brown and her children might gain the luxury of a dream. Jessie might dream that some day there really could be curtains at her windows. Ten-year old Clyde's dreaming might be of a bicycle instead of a bowl of oatmeal for breakfast. Two-year old Ruby, who is perhaps not old enough to dream, might gain in her brown eyes some of the happiness of security that I see in the faces of my own children and their friends.

Twelve families. I wonder if they could be found in the Kennebunks? After discounting the families who would not give because they believe that charity begins at home (and yet don't seek out a Jessie Brown in Maine), and those who would lack the conviction that helping one needy family would make any difference in view of the thousands who need help, and those who would promise to give and then would forget, and those families who couldn't give — would there still be twelve families in the Kennebunks who would give that dollar a week? They must exist within the boundaries of my world, but where are they? Twelve familes to care about one family. How can they be found? Are they alive and thinking? Jessie Brown is.

thunderstorm

It seemed to me that dusk had come early. I looked up from my preoccupation with cleaning the kitchen after supper and saw that the light of day had faded and the gloom of evening had settled in. Even considering that the long light of midsummer already wanes earlier each day as the summer season leans to fall, it seemed that this day had ended surprisingly early. And then I realized that a storm was brewing.

I stood at the open kitchen window looking out into the yard. The air was still. The heavy, brooding heat of late afternoon had gone; the air was cool, but it was still. The flowers stood tall in the garden, etched red and orange against the green shrubbery. They waited like dancers poised at the beginning of a dance, and even as I watched a gentle breeze sprang up and set them and the leaves of the shrubbery and trees moving in graceful motion. The breeze brought the smell of summer to me: the scent of green grass, warm dirt, of the heat of the day, and of lemon lilies, phlox and all growing things.

I went out onto the porch and looked up into the sky. Grey, white-rimmed clouds seethed across the sky, roiled by a wind that swept suddenly into the yard where the tall trees leaned, and sighed, and threw down their first dead leaves. The yellow leaves went skidding across the grass and tangled themselves in the feet of the flowers. The tall stalks of purple loosestrife waved and the first rain patterned the flagstone path as purple-throated thunder grumbled ominously in the distance, and the cats scurried for cover.

Somewhere there was light; behind the clouds, but their layers diffused it to a thin brightness like a wash of silver. As the rain came heavier the silver dulled to pewter-grey, and the flowers in the long gardens were misted out of shape even though their colors were still vivid. Only the heavy lines of the spruce trees, tall beyond the gardens, remained distinct, and they seemed drawn in India ink against the flat sky. Now and again lightning flashed its white line across the sky and for a moment the gathering gloom was lifted.

I sat on the porch and watched the rain and felt its mist on my face and arms. In its vigor it washed away the scent of the lemon lilies and left instead its own clean, wet smell. It rushed in the downspout of the drain, and I sat listening to its rush and racket until the early dusk was covered by black night and it was time to sleep.

up country

Yesterday we drove into Maine. We did not go "down east," following the coastline to salty villages by the sea; rather, we drove "up country" toward lakes and farms. It was a warm morning, and we wondered at the wisdom of heading inland on such a day, but our purpose in going was to take Aunt Dotty to look at a piece of waterfront property that was for sale, and the owner was expecting us that afternoon. We packed a picnic lunch: roast chicken, stuffed eggs, pickles, fruit and lemonade, with a striped cloth to spread it on, and bright napkins, plates, and cups to match. We packed our bathing suits too, and promised the children a swim in a lake.

We started out by turnpike, enjoying the view on either side of lush green fields filled with dancing daisies and the haze of blue vetch. Our mood was light, and we joined the children in singing nonsense songs.

We left the turnpike at Gray, picnicked at a pine-scented, State-maintained rest area, and then continued on, following secondary roads to the town that was our destination. There were signs of change in the town although it still had the flavor that, while not Colonial-sea-captain's-village, is yet typically old Maine. The main street was wide. We passed a new long, low school, its lawn planted with sapling trees. We passed a new bank and post office; neat brick buildings of Colonial design with white trim. But most of the buildings in the business center of the town were not new. The doorways to the stores were up a granite step or two from the sidewalk, and the nature of their business was only subtly adver- tised by old-fashioned signs: "A. P. Blodgett-Hardware." I suspected that the interior of "Green's Market" smelled of freshly ground coffee, dill pickles, and strong cheese, and I wondered if a Victorian leaded-glass lamp hung in the drugstore or if it had been replaced by a fluorescent light.

We stopped at a gas station that, like the town, was in transi- tion. Behind the small, clapboarded building a larger one of ce- ment block construction was going up. A thick old vine grew up over the doorway of the wooden building. I was sorry to think that it would have to be cut down to make room for a pair of shiny new gas pumps.

The business district evolved gradually into the residential dis- trict. The houses were Victorian in style with turrets supporting little pointed, bracketed roofs, and big, square windows topped with panels of stained glass. They had wide, front porches draped with broad-leaved vines. I thought about sitting on one of those porches, smelling the scent of summer and hearing the sound of a screen door slamming at the back of the cool, dim interior of the house.

But our business did not lie in the town, and we left it, crossing a river, passing a lumber mill, and so into the countryside. We were looking for the house of a man named Arthur Fickett. He liv- ed on the Chase's Ridge Road. We found the road and followed it up along the ridge where cool breezes brought the smell of old cow manure to us. This was farm country, but it no longer prospered. The fields were full of wild flowers and the barns we passed were falling into disrepair, no longer needed by the farmers who had sold their cows and worked in the town. Old stone walls followed the road. They had been built to mark boun- daries, or to keep cows in, or simply to get the stones out of the fields so corn could be planted. Their beauty was accidental, and although their function was gone, they, like the smell of manure, would endure for a time.

We came to Arthur Fickett's farm. The house needed painting, and the roof of the ell was falling in. A clothes line was strung on the front porch and a load of firewood was dumped by the steps.

Bob and Aunt Dotty went to the door, but the children and I crossed the road to wander around the barn.

We found that it was no longer used except by swallows who
wheeled and swooped above us when we pushed aside a
Wirthmore feed bag that hung over one of the windows, and looked in. The interior of the barn was open to the sky, for the roof
had fallen in. Wood sorrel had sprouted from the moist, elemental
richness of the rotting roof timbers and floor boards.

"Look, Charlotte's web," cried Stephanie, remembering a
favorite story when she saw a spider web spanning old timbers.
Beside the barn was a pond edged in buttercups. A few ducks
swam there, and a dragonfly flew past, beating his wings over the
water.

We returned to the house and found Arthur Fickett standing in
the yard talking with Bob and Dot. He was a heavyset man whose
brawn was running to fat although he was not yet middle-aged.
He needed a shave and his T-shirt and tan pants were dirty with
the dirt of yesterday's work. He talked in a flat all-of-a-kind voice
and although his expression was non-commital I felt that our
measure was being taken. He was speaking of the land we had
come to see.

"That lot's on a point of land. Most expensive lot down there,
but o'course there's room to put two houses on it, side by side, if
you stay friends." We offered no comment, and wanting to
emphasize his point he added, "S'long's you don't get mad at
one'nother you could put two houses on that point of land." Then
with deliberation and as if settling in for a good long chat he
dropped down on one knee on the grass, crossed his wrists one on
the other, resting them on his knee, and squinting through the
smoke of a cigarette he held between his fingers he asked, "Where
you folks from?"

"Kennebunk," Bob told him. He nodded and said, "Heard o'
that place. Never been there myself. I saw that singer woman on
TV. She's got a house there. Got blueberries, I believe." Ah yes,
Jane Morgan Blueberries from Blueberry Hill in Kennebunkport.

When at last we were able to cut into his talk to ask how we
could get to the pond to look at the lot he said, "Take that road
over there." He pointed to a raw dirt track that ran off through
the field on the other side of the road. "M'brother's down there.
He'll show y'around." As we turned to go he added, "Just follow
the signs."

The "road" to the pond crossed an old pasture which was
strewn with boulders and clumps of juniper. Here and there stood
a piece of rusty farm machinery, forgotten, waiting to be thought

about or needed. We came to the first sign almost immediately. It was nailed to a post which stood by the pasture brook where a few planks had been laid down to serve as a bridge. The sign said "Fickett's Bridge, Erected 1966." On past the "bridge" the road went up and then suddenly down and into a scattering of young evergreens. Indian paint brush grew in an orange band between the road and the trees.

The road lumped its way over a flat rock and past a sign that said "Road Closed Per Order of the Selectmen." It seemed that that would not be a bad idea, but we continued on and found that the signs did indeed lead us. "Western Union Telegraph" proclaimed one and "Rest Room" we read in the middle of nowhere. We came into a small clearing and read "No U Turn" and "No Parking." By the time we came to the sign that said "Charter Bus Service Here" we had caught the spirit of the thing and laughed aloud. After a particularly bad stretch of road we came to a sign that said "Slow — End of Improved Section." The next sign, "We Have Built The Better Mousetrap," made me wonder if it marked the site of a springtime mud hole. At last we could go no further. Trees barred the way, and a sign said "Stop."

A few steps away we found Arthur Fickett's brother at his camp, which sat in a clearing on the edge of the pond. A sign nailed to a tree in the yard said "No Hunting," and as he led us off to show us the lot that was for sale I noticed a sign over the outhouse door. It said "Public Telephone."

We walked the lot, happy to find clumps of birch trees standing along the water's edge. We found strawberries in the underbrush and deer tracks and droppings in the soft dirt. We listened to the sound of the water lapping on the stones that edged the shore and smelled sun-warmed fresh water and old pine.

Arthur's brother told us that there were white perch in the pond and good hunting in the woods in the fall. He suggested that all one would need to do was clear out the alders to have a good view of the water. At last, perhaps gaining confidence in us, he said, "We kind of hope somebody will come in here who'll like the place pretty much as it is and won't want to stir things up too much." This was no problem: Dotty had come seeking peace not progress.

No deals were made yesterday, but I suspect one is in the offing. I hope so. I'd like to go back; to drive into Maine where the out-of-date softens hard, bright progress; to chat with Arthur Fickett and his brother and to chuckle my way down their road. Aunt Dotty would put a simple camp on that point of land and let the wild strawberries and the deer come up to the front door. There would be a little boat for fishing in the pond and when the wind blew off the water it would turn the leaves on the birch trees and shake them all together, and something would be satisfied in those of us lucky enough to hear their sound.

the ritual

I am about to perform the Old New England ritual of Fall Housecleaning. I shall scrub, scour, dust and disrupt every room in this house. I shall empty out and reorganize every closet, cupboard, and drawer. I shall weed out our possessions, making contributions to the Goodwill box and the dump. I shall begin on Monday.

MONDAY: Woke to a beautiful sunny morning. Resisted an impulse to take a bicycle ride and began my housecleaning. Started with the living room. Took down the gold drapes and hung them on the line to air. Scrubbed all the woodwork. Washed the windows (75 small panes of glass). Took the fins off the baseboard radiators and vacuumed the grillwork. Washed the mantlepiece. Emptied the ashes out of the fireplace, washed the hearth and waxed the bricks. Moved all the furniture, vacuumed the rug, and washed the border of painted floor. Polished the furniture. Emptied out the drawers of the chest and desk. Sorted everything, saving only those items worth saving, which seemed to be just about everything. Put all the loose snapshots in a box and will spend a winter afternoon pasting them into albums (lost half an hour here looking at the children's baby pictures and remembering). Emptied the closet beside the fireplace. Sorted everything. Threw out old catalogues. Set aside pamphlets ("How to Raise Raspberries," "How to Avoid Financial Tangles") to be carried to a filing cabinet in the attic. Set games aside to be stored in the closet in the family room. Couldn't decide what to do with some things (a bell of Sarna, a camera that needs repair, coin wrappers) so put them back in the closet. Polished the brass latch on the closet door and the fireplace fixtures. Managed to rehang the drapes before the children arrived home from school. Was asked at the supper table how I spent my day, and felt somewhat vexed that the question needed asking.

TUESDAY: Tackled the family room today. I use the verb advisedly. We really live in that room, and it is there that we keep our collections of old bottles and antique tools and our books. Loaded the bottles into the dishwasher with the breakfast dishes. Took all the books down from the floor to ceiling shelves, stacking them everywhere. Washed the shelves and began putting the books back by category: history, poetry, art, etc. This was time consuming, and desultory reading didn't speed up the process. Spent some time with Durant's *Age of Faith.* Read in *Crime and Punishment,* and enjoyed a foray into Hopkins' poetry. Skimmed Freuchen's *Book of the Seven Seas* while eating a very late lunch. After my sandwich, made fairly good progress until I got to *Hitty: Her First Hundred Years.* The children arrived home before I could finish the books. "What happened?" they asked, looking in amazement at the drift of reading material spread on every chair and across the floor. Tonight I was not asked what I had done with today.

WEDNESDAY: Finished the family room today. Couldn't find room in the closet for all the games so carried some to the attic. Vacuumed the furniture, and under the cushions of the couch found six pennies, four crayons, two pencils, and a peanut from our last birthday party peanut hunt. Tonight my pleasure in contemplating the neatly organized books, the sparkling array of bottles, the polished tools, and the glow of firelight on the beautifully waxed and buffed pine floor helped me to forget the disruption of the dining room where curtains are down and silver awaits polishing.

THURSDAY: 9:30 p.m. Have just finished ironing and hanging the last dining room curtain. That room is finished, but must admit I do not feel satisfied with it. I should repaint the chipped and scratched floor, but I'm not going to do it.

FRIDAY: "Whatever is worth doing is worth doing well." Lord Chesterfield said it, but it is also a Yankee adage. I'm a Yankee born and bred. Painted the dining room floor this morning. After lunch I started cleaning the kitchen. Suppertime found the contents of the food cupboards and all the pots and pans still waiting to be put away, and the cleaning of the oven only half done. Supper came out of cans, and as we ate our Campbell's soup, surrounded on all sides by clutter, and sniffing the smell of wet paint, Jamie asked scornfully, "Is *this* Fall Housecleaning?"

SATURDAY: Set the children to work this morning sorting the clutter in their rooms. Gave them each a large box for those possessions they were willing to send to the dump. I worked in the kitchen. Soon discovered that the boxes were still relatively empty and drawers and cupboards still full so sent the children out to play and tackled the job myself. Made great progress, but the children came in periodically to check the boxes, and old dolls, trucks without wheels, school papers, and empty chocolate boxes found their way back into drawers. Did manage to spirit a few mendable toys into the attic (to be given away at Christmas time for repair and distribution to needy children), and also weeded out a few coloring books. We have saved every coloring book that ever came into this house. Educators who frown on coloring books — believing that they interfere with natural creative processes — would not be impressed with our collection. While I do not agree with the educators, I do believe that a time should come when a coloring book can be thrown away. Threw out the Cinderella books and a few others. I am tired tonight and shall be in bed before the children are asleep.

SUNDAY: Sunday is a day of rest and it is also dump day. My week's activity had filled the dump barrels to overflowing. Spent a good part of the afternoon reading the *New York Times*. A letter to the editor sent me looking for last week's paper, and I discovered that it had been carried to the dump. At that point Stephanie came asking if I had seen her Cinderella coloring book. We consoled each other.

MONDAY: Spent today on the upstairs. In Jamie's room I sorted toys. Tinker Toys, Legos and Lincoln Logs went back into the toy box, and a great armload of bedraggled, stuffed animals went into the attic, but one cache of horse chestnuts, bubble gum wrappers, wheels from miniature cars, and popsicle sticks went untouched because I did not know what was trash and what treasure. I cleaned the girls' room thoroughly except for the doll house. If *that* house is to have a Fall Housecleaning they must do it.

TUESDAY: The Bible says of the industrious housewife: "Her children rise up and call her blessed; her husband also, and he praiseth her." I don't think my family feels that way. They suffer. The cookie jar is empty, and the ironing basket is full.

WEDNESDAY: I rehung the last clean curtain in our bedroom today and triumphantly announced aloud, "There, I'm done!" But a little later, upon carrying a load of out-of-season clothes to the attic I realized that while I might be "done-in" I was not finished. Instead of weeding our possessions *out* I have been weeding them *up*. The attic is in chaos.

THURSDAY: It rained today, and I was glad to be in the attic to hear the counterpoint on the roof. I spent the day there, and while

I did make some firm decisions in favor of the Goodwill box and the dump, there was much that I simply packed away again. Yellow stacks of Geographics, old and quaint books, 78 RPM records, and a trunk full of patchwork pieces belong in an attic. Last year's Halloween masks, May baskets and valentines, old letters and scrapbooks, baby clothes, football sweaters and Navy jackets smelling of mothballs belong in an attic too, and these relics are best thrown out by a stranger to them.

FRIDAY: Did not sleep well last night. Dreamed of the old friends and places that were called to mind during my rummaging in the attic. Eve the Cat did not appear for breakfast. Found her in the attic when I went up to finish my work.

SATURDAY: My Fall Housecleaning is finished. Someone spilled orange juice on the kitchen floor this morning, and the dust has settled in the living room again, but if one must continually clean a house, at least ordinary housework does leave time for the amenities of homemaking. I set bread to rise this morning and put an arrangement of dried grasses on the dining room table. The fall swag hangs on the front door, and pumpkins sit on the steps. Let the year turn; my house is ready.

article 8

I went to the special town meeting last night. I went to support Article 8 which asked that the selectmen be authorized to borrow $85,000 to begin a drastic program to prevent the spread of Dutch Elm disease, which is ravaging the elm trees of Kennebunk. The program called for the removal and burial of dead elm trees, and the pruning of dead limbs from partially infected trees. This sanitation program, the most effective type of program for controlling the spread of the disease, was to be carried out in a control area. The program also included the planting of new trees. As I climbed the steps into the Town Hall I felt optimistic that at last Kennebunk would be able to save some of her elms.

The meeting was well attended and most of the almost five hours we spent in the hall was devoted to Article 8. The discussion was emotional and involved and out of it came an amendment, put forth by Mr. Marshall, that limited the funds to be borrowed to $25,000 and restricted their use to the removal of dead trees. The amendment specified that only dead trees bordering town ways should be removed (those set back from the road on private property were not to be touched) and the trees must be cut down all over Kennebunk and not just in a control area. No funds would be spent for the pruning of partially infected trees, and there would be no planting program. Adoption of the amendment would mean that Kennebunk would not be making any effort to stop the spread of the disease, but would simply be starting the job of removing trees already dead.

I voted against the amendment. It passed. I also voted against the amended article hoping that if no funds were voted the matter would have to come before the townspeople again and perhaps a larger appropriation than the $25,000 and some control measures could be voted. Article 8 as amended passed.

We voted by secret ballot instead of by a show of hands. The voting and the counting of the ballots took a long time, so after casting my ballot I did not return to my seat, but went to stand by an open window. The hall was stuffy and the doors had been locked until the balloting was over. The window was only raised a foot so I bent over and put my face to the opening, breathing the fine night air. Across the street huge elm trees were illuminated by the street lights. I peered up at the canopy of their limbs wondering if they were still healthy and if so would beetles fly to them next spring from a winter nest in a dead tree in someone's back yard.

I think I believed that the amended article would fail until I heard that it had not. I stood with the cold air on my back and heard the moderator read the results. The vote was 132 for, 87 against. I felt heartsick and said aloud, "I'm sick about this." A man standing nearby said, "Why? We've voted $25,000. We'll spend that and make a start and then see what's to be done."

"But it will be too late. The beetles nest in dead trees, and they'll fly in the spring and infect healthy trees."

"Oh, really?" he said. He hadn't known that.

I had no heart for the rest of the meeting and went out into the vestibule. A few people stood in a group talking. One of them was Mr. Marshall. As I entered the vestibule a man who had taken his wife home to relieve a baby sitter came in. He had voted, but had not heard the results. "How did it go?" he asked.

"We won," Mr. Marshall said. "They can only spend $25,000, and the important thing is dead trees are to be cut down all over town, not just in one area."

"Good," said a woman. "That's as it should be." It was too much for me. In my agitation I broke into their conversation.

"But don't you see," I said, pounding my fist on the table. "You've got to have a control area to stop the disease from spreading. What is Kennebunk without her elms? I feel sick about it. You don't realize what you've done. You don't realize." Mr. Marshall looked at me with surprise and with what seemed to be a mixture of resignation and a touch of compassion. It seemed that he was about to speak, but the sounds of the meeting inside floated out to us, and as I turned away from him he headed back into the hall. In a moment I heard his voice inside, raised in question of the article under discussion.

Today I still feel heartsick. I had hoped the people of Kennebunk would band together to save their elm trees with a drastic appropriation. They did not, and I wonder why. I wonder if the elms were sacrificed because people are uninformed. I wonder if they were sacrificed because money is more important in our lives than anything. I wonder if the elms were the pawns in a power struggle, or if they were sacrificed for lack of an articulate and impassioned spokesman. Or if they were lost because, as one man said to me, "Kennebunk abrogated her right to elm trees years ago when she didn't care enough to spend enough to fight the disease."

In answer to this argument and all the others like it I heard at the meeting, I think about the insurmountable odds men have faced in this world in order to salvage something they valued: the Egyptian temples along the Nile, the priceless manuscripts and art treasures of Florence. I wonder if I am being dramatic in comparing the elms of Kennebunk, Maine, with mankind's cultural inheritance, but elm trees are a part of the inheritance of New Englanders, and seeing them one gains the same perspective on the human estate that great art gives.

I drove into the village today, and as I rode down Summer Street I looked carefully to see just how many trees of other species I could see standing with the great dead, dying, and vulnerable elms. I saw very few, and none were as tall as the elms or spread their limbs as far.

neighborhoods

If things continue as they are going we might have a Neighborhood someday soon. Jamie has recently met Tommy, who lives on the other side of the woods, and sometimes when Tommy comes to play he brings his friend Mark. Pam lives on the corner, and she is Leslie's friend. Suellen, Stephanie's friend, lives up the road within walking distance and she has 3 brothers: David, Billy, and Peter. We have always invited children from across town to come and play, but this depends on parental transportation and a Neighborhood requires instant mobility and long periods of uninterrupted play that don't hinge on adult schedules and whim. The child who lives in a neighborhood of children leads a rich and creative daily existence.

I speak of Neighborhoods from experience. I grew up in one. There were three of us Kelley kids: Joan, John and Joyce. Our best friends were the Spofford children: Jeanette, Randy and Doris. We six were only a small part of the large number of children who lived in our area.

I have many memories of our escapades, most of them happy and satisfying, but over some of them hangs the spectre of Mrs. Moore. Mrs. Moore didn't have any children of her own. She didn't understand children or enjoy them. We kids called her "Old Lady Moore," and if this sounds disrespectful it was perhaps justified in light of the fact that she set herself up as our enemy. Old Lady Moore did not want us in or near her neatly kept yard. She did not appreciate our noise, our numbers, or our activities. She often threatened to tell our parents on us (which she frequently did), and on more than one occasion she threatened to call the police. We lived in fear of the day when she *would* call the police and tried to stay out of her range, which was very hard to do, for she seemed to make all of our business her business.

One summer day when Doris and I were playing house with our dolls and dishes Joan and Jeanette came running to tell us, "Come on. We're going to have a parade. Charlie Goodrich found a box of costumes in his attic, and we're going to have a circus parade." Doris and I jumped up.

"We want to be beautiful ladies," said Doris. Wearing high heels and grown-up finery was one of our favorite pastimes.

"You can't," said our older sisters, who were always bossing us around. "We're going to do that so you've got to be something else." As it turned out Doris and I were clowns and wore a matching pair of gaudy bloomers and funny hats and . . . high heels.

When the call went out in our Neighborhood for a really fun project it was not difficult to collect a large number of children. I think twenty or more of us gathered for that parade, and what a parade it was. We augmented the costumes from Charlie Goodrich's attic with all the hats and paraphernalia we could find, and at least one dog was put on a long rope and became a lion. Two or three other dogs ran freely beside us barking accompaniment to the music we made with young voices, pots and pans, and whistles.

We paraded all around our Neighborhood. Aproned mothers came out on porches to laugh us on our way, and handymen, the mailman, and the storekeeper stopped their work to smile us by. We had a wonderful time. But the day was hot, our route was long, and our pride in our cleverness impaired our judgment: we stopped to rest in Old Lady Moore's field.

Mrs. Moore's field bordered on her yard. Ordinarily we avoided stepping so much as one foot on her property, but we were hot and tired and our success made us bold, so when our parade route brought us to Old Lady Moore's house and our leader, one of the older boys, suggested that we stop to rest in the field, we complied. We spilled off the sidewalk into the tall, sweet-smelling grass. We sat and lay in the field, happily discussing our wonderful costumes and parade. Hats were off and defenses down when suddenly someone said, "Look!" and pointed toward Old Lady Moore's house. There she was, standing on her porch, writing on a pad of paper. As we watched she raised her hand and began to count us.

"What's she doing?"

"She's written down our names."

"What's she going to do?"

"She's going to *call the police!*"

"We'd better get out of here. They'll come and put us in jail."

"Run! Run and hide." Some of the little ones began to cry and all of us were afraid. We ran. We ran in all directions, pulling off our costumes as we went, noses running, hearts pounding, tripping on long skirts and falling out of high heels.

We didn't know where to run. How can you escape when you've been seen? Some of us, crying and sweating, stumbled at last into Charlie Goodrich's yard, not sure whether to stay, to head for the woods, or for home. As we stood in indecision one of the big kids said, "Aw, I don't think she was going to call the police at all."

"Oh yeah! Well why was she writing our names down then?" The scoffer had no answer, but he had courage. "I'll go ask her," he said.

"You don't dare."

"I do too." Off he went.

We were aghast at his daring and sat in morbid curiosity waiting for his return from such peril. Indeed, we wondered if he *would* return or if he would be carried off by the police to pay the debt all of us had incurred by sitting in Mrs. Moore's field. But return he did, swaggering, sneering, and proclaiming, "She wasn't going to call the police. She was going to call the *newspaper*. She was going to have them come out to take our picture for the paper. She thought we was great! Stupid kids. Scaredy cats. You spoiled everything. We could've had our pictures in the paper."

We were stunned. Great was our sense of loss and frustration at missing such as opportunity. Great was our confusion as the full realization came to us that Old Lady Moore had actually appreciated our parade. Even now it is difficult for me to accept that fact, and in light of it I still wonder, as I did then, what Mrs. Moore thought when that defiant boy rang her bell and asked, "Was you going to call the police on us?"

Neighborhoods are exciting, as any child who has grown out of one can tell you, and they provide an education in living as well as rich memories. But it takes a lot of kids to make a Neighborhood with perhaps just a few adults available to make things interesting.

thanksgiving

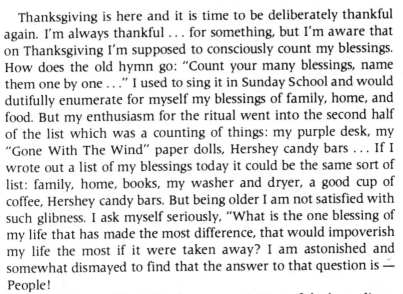

Thanksgiving is here and it is time to be deliberately thankful again. I'm always thankful ... for something, but I'm aware that on Thanksgiving I'm supposed to consciously count my blessings. How does the old hymn go: "Count your many blessings, name them one by one ..." I used to sing it in Sunday School and would dutifully enumerate for myself my blessings of family, home, and food. But my enthusiasm for the ritual went into the second half of the list which was a counting of things: my purple desk, my "Gone With The Wind" paper dolls, Hershey candy bars ... If I wrote out a list of my blessings today it could be the same sort of list: family, home, books, my washer and dryer, a good cup of coffee, Hershey candy bars. But being older I am not satisfied with such glibness. I ask myself seriously, "What is the one blessing of my life that has made the most difference, that would impoverish my life the most if it were taken away? I am astonished and somewhat dismayed to find that the answer to that question is — People!

How can I possibly make that answer? Most of the hurt, disappointment, frustration and anger in my life has been because of people. The hurt and disappointment came early with the first snub by a childhood best friend, and recurred through the years when adults didn't care enough or at the right times, with the loss of high school beaus, and with misunderstandings and conflicts with college and community peers. I have been frustrated by people who have been, by my standards, thoughtless, selfish, insensitive, uncommitted. I have been angry with liars and litter bugs, bigots, insolent youths, egotists, and opportunists. I have considered people the bane of my existence and a plague on the earth.

How can I count people as my greatest blessing when it is also true that no person of my acquaintance needs people less than I do? I am basically an introvert and need all the time I can get to think my own thoughts, pursue my own interests, work on my own projects. I have resented demands made on me by family and friends. I have said more than once, when working in some organization, "This job would be easy and a pleasure if only I didn't have to work with people." All of my life people have interfered with my fussy I and my creative self.

There are, of course, easy answers. It is obvious that living without people would be like gardening without plants. The pleasures of books, music, antiques, theater, wine, art, clothes, food . . . of everything . . . come from people. The joys of good conversation, of laughing, of loving are possible because of people. People, not things, enrich life.

People have enriched my life not only with pleasure, but by giving me direction. By being themselves people have shown me what I wanted to be as well as what I did *not* want to be. People have made demands on me that I would never have dared to make on myself so that often when I have achieved personal success it has been because someone asked me to try for it.

People have also released me from the vacuum of self. To live in a small town is, if one is really a part of the life of the town, to belong to organizations and to serve on committees. Although most of us become involved in the beginning for personal reasons — our own pleasure or status — we soon discover that committee work takes too much time and energy to be continued for such frivolous reasons. We find ourselves staying involved because we care about whether or not little girls can be Girl Scouts, about good books for the library, about good government in the town, about pollution in the rivers, about activities for the very old and the teenagers, about whether or not Sunday School keeps. We are working for people when we serve on these committees.

We get tired of the work. We get fed up, and we say, "I'm all done. No more. I'm going to stay home and mind my own business and enjoy life." But that is when we discover how much we care. We find ourselves becoming involved in issues we don't wish to face, of working on committees when we are too tired to work, of caring when we don't want to care. And I have found that being concerned is not a sometime emotion: it builds, it accumulates until you end up caring about all states and stages of human existence.

People are the greatest blessing of my life. I care about people, all kinds of people, even those I don't like, even bigots and Yippies and opportunists and despoilers. That sounds pious. I'm sorry that it does because I don't feel at all pious. Instead I feel rather grim. It is a terrible burden. I don't understand why, but it is a burden that I carry.

On this Thanksgiving Day, in this year of war, racism, riots, moratoriums, pollution, pornography, famine and crime, I shall count my greatest blessing as people. God help me.

green memories

If only we could distill Christmas. If only we could bring its richness down and gain its essence. If only we could savor Christmas as we can savor a fine wine. Thinking carefully I realize that of course we can. We savor Christmas through our memories.

Christmas sprawls and overflows. It is made up of too many catalogues in the mail, too many shopping trips, and too many cards to be sent. Christmas is boxes of ornaments on the dining room table waiting to be placed on the tree and mantle. It is the card table in the front room overflowing with wrapping paper and ribbon. It is more presents than there are hiding places in the house. It is more tins of cookies than there is room for on the pantry shelf, and too many fairs, parties, and pageants. But from all of this richness we draw the memories that make us say, "Oh, I love Christmas." And through remembering we gain the essence of the holiday.

I remember. I remember feeling very small in a big bed on Christmas Eve and trying not to go to sleep until I heard Santa's bells at the top of the house and being suddenly afraid, because I thought I *had* heard his bells.

I remember finding a bottle of Blue Waltz perfume in my stocking on all the Christmas mornings of my youth. I remember the year I had five dollars to buy my presents for the family. I went into McClellen's Dime Store and spent the afternoon choosing the perfect gift for each one: a white Bible for Joan, a blue satin pillow for Nicky's bed, hankies for Dad, a knife for John, a large bottle of carnation bath salts for Mama, a horn for Bobby. That was the first Christmas I was more concerned with the gifts I was giving than the gifts I was to receive.

I remember the family party the year I was twelve, and being asked by a cousin what I'd gotten for presents. I listed all my grand gifts. Grammy King, whom I hadn't noticed sitting nearby, asked, "And did you get the apron I made for you?" I felt uncomfortable and sorry that I hadn't named the apron, for I realized then that it was all she had to give. Some of the glitter went out of Christmas that year, but it was the kind of glitter that could be spared.

I remember the Christmas of the year we had all gone away from home to study or to work. On Christmas Eve we gathered together and sitting around the tree we decided suddenly to drive over to where Grammy King was living to sing carols for her. Grammy was in bed, and we crowded into her room finding a place to stand amid the clutter of the rocking chair that had always stood in her dining room, the book case that held Grampy King's books, the tables covered with pictures of her children and grandchildren. We stood tall and important in our youth and sang in our strong voices, "O come all ye faithful, joyful and triumphant . . ." Grammy sang with us in her thin voice. Looking at her white hair and her patient hands on the spread I felt warm and happy and wonderfully close to everyone in that room. Being old and sick and done with Christmas surprises for rosy toddlers and Christmas dinners for strong sons was the best Christmas present Grammy King ever gave to me.

I remember the year I was working in the college bookstore with Mrs. Proctor. On the last day of classes before the Christmas recess I asked her if she was looking forward to hearing the students sing carols from the steps of the library that evening.

"No," she said. "My son, who was killed in the war, was reported missing in action on December 19th and to this day I can't bear to hear the carols." I thought of her that star-lit night as I stood on the steps of the library with my friends and sang "Silent night, holy night . . .," and I wondered how she could face the coming of Christmas year after year.

After I was married I came home for Christmas to Mother Butler's house. I remember the colored balls she hung in each window pane and the warmth of the lights and her greeting streaming out into the frosty night to meet us. She taught me about making Christmas traditions. Every year she put the Bible on the mantle with greens on either side and a red ribbon marking St. Luke, Chapter II. And there was always plum pudding and lemon curd for Christmas dinner. She is dead now, and we are still learning to have Christmas without her, but much of what Christmas is in our house is because of her.

I remember Christmases with our children. I remember the year Aunt Bertha and I made gingerbread men, carefully giving each one raisin eyes and buttons. I remember how Stephanie, who was three, followed behind our busy backs and carefully ate each raisin.

The year Jamie was five we took him to the Christmas Eve service with us and he was restless, missing the beauty of the candlelit sanctuary. He amused himself by smiling at his golden haired friend, Letitia, who sat in the next pew with her family. But before the service was over she fell asleep, her yellow head leaning against her mother's arm, innocently beautiful in the candlelight. And then Jamie was quiet, content to look at her, and some of the magic of that place and moment came to him.

These are my Christmas memories. Everyone has such memories. They come to us when we bring out a favorite ornament, hear the carols, taste a Christmas bread. Remembering a time that is gone, a person we will never see again, a place we can never go back to, we savor Christmas even as we rush about creating the memories of another year. If I were to make a prayer for December 25 I would say: Give us this day our Christmas joy; our wassailing around the tinseled tree; the warmth of hearth and drink and friend; the cheer of children; the pain of the old, the sick, the lonely; and give us, please, a "green memory."*

*Charles Dickens, "Lord, Keep My Memory Green."

the christmas miracle

There are cookies to be made, cards to be addressed, packages to be wrapped, and I have spent my day making a Santa Claus suit for Talking Tammy. Talking Tammy is an 18" doll with freckles, and she is going to be Santa in a puppet show Leslie's 5th grade class is going to present at school. My list of holiday projects did not include making a suit for Tammy. Goodness knows I already had enough to do to get ready for Christmas, but Leslie promised her classmates a Santa for the play and sometimes it is important for mothers to help their children to fullfill promises.

Happily the materials I needed came readily to hand and my fingers worked with an unaccustomed dexterity. I found a piece of bright red wool in the material drawer and a square of black felt (for boots and a belt) in the felt box. I found cotton batting (fur to trim coat, hat and boots) in the bathroom supply closet, and a bathrobe pattern for a 15" doll turned out to be a perfect coat size for Tammy. When the button drawer in the old sewing machine offered up a miniature, gold belt buckle it seemed that perhaps Providence or Fate or the Spirit of Christmas was at work in our midst. That the Spirit of Christmas would concern himself with Tammy was probable, for Tammy is a Christmas doll and the year she came is remembered as the year we witnessed a minor Christmas miracle.

Leslie was five years old the year Santa brought her Talking Tammy. Santa had brought a doll every Christmas, but always a baby doll in a high chair or a small doll with homemade clothes and a bed from Daddy's workshop with a homemade mattress, featherstitched sheets and a patchwork quilt. Tammy was something different. She was what I call a Commercial Doll, a doll heavily advertised by the manufacturer. In fact, Tammy was a talking doll! A ring dangled from her back and when it was pulled, from inside her sturdy body a childish voice said, "I'm hungry" or "I love you." Every little girl, or her mother, wanted Tammy. But Tammy's cost was prohibitive, which was a comfort to me, an old-fashioned mother who believed in baby dolls with homemade clothes. Leslie loved her baby dolls, but the Tammys who belonged to her friends were tantalizing, and Tammy never ceased to be desirable even when the manufacturer ignored her and concentrated his selling efforts on a walking doll.

The Christmas that Leslie was five I found a store selling Tammy at a discount price and, thinking that finding her under the tree would put stars in Leslie's eyes, I bought her. Great was my excitement and satisfaction the day I brought her home and secreted her in the barn attic, an unheated chamber where little girls were not allowed because of the cold. In the days that followed, as I made Christmas in our house, I imagined Leslie's joy when she came downstairs Christmas morning to find that Santa had, at last, brought the talking doll. My pleasure in anticipating the scene filled each day of that last Christmas week with the glow of Christmas morning.

The day before Christmas was a cold, bright day that blued off early into evening. Stockings were hung by the chimney carefully and the children hurried off to bed to lie awake listening for Santa. We adults sat by the glowing tree to wait until sleep overcame their excitement so that Santa could come. The evening leaned toward midnight when at last we began Santa's work, bringing out the gaily wrapped packages from hiding places all over the house. Tammy came last, down from the cold attic, into the

Christmas room. I lifted her out of her box, smoothed her yellow hair, studied her freckled face — deciding it was a wholesome face — and then before sitting her under the tree, I pulled her talking string.

The joy of Christmas is fragile if it is predicated on the false. My joy in Christmas vanished when I pulled that string, for as it reluctantly wound itself back into the doll the only sound produced was a dull grinding of gears. Tammy did not talk. Tammy couldn't talk, as repeated tries proved. I undressed her to see if there was some way to get at her talking box. There was none. I ran my fingers in frustration over the plastic webbing that covered her malfunctioning motor and felt like the child who has lost his penny down a grating in the sidewalk. Except it was Leslie's Christmas I had lost. Tammy was Santa's gift. How could I explain to her that Santa's gift was less than perfect? I couldn't tell her that Tammy came from a discount store that had offered her at a cut rate because she was imperfect (how else explain this early loss of her voice)? And what could we do at midnight on Christmas Eve with a talking doll that couldn't talk? There was nothing we could do except dress Tammy, sit her under the tree and go to bed dreading the morning that was coming.

It seemed a long night because I woke often afraid that it was over. The children were up before the sun, and I was thankful that in our house Santa left the filled stockings on the end of their beds. The ritual of emptying the stockings delayed going downstairs to see what Santa had left under the tree. But the moment came. Leslie led the way. I followed slowly at the end of the procession, steeling myself for the disappointment, seeking vainly for the plausible explanation that hadn't yet come to mind.

The children burst into the Christmas room.

"Talking Tammy," Leslie cried. "Santa brought me Talking Tammy." She picked up the doll and reached for the ring.

"I'm hungry," said Tammy.

"She talked!" I cried in amazement. "She talked!"

"Of course, Mama," said Leslie importantly. "Tammy is a talking doll."

Christmas is a time for miracles. Some are minor, like our miracle of the talking doll, but they are important nevertheless. Understanding the mechanics of a miracle does not make it any less important either.

Tammy doesn't talk anymore. Leslie wore her out rather quickly, and she became just another doll whose voice is heard in her mistress's imagination. I'm rather glad that Leslie picked her to be Santa in the play because from now on she will be Santa in our house every year, sitting near the tree in her homemade Santa suit, and seeing her I will remember our Christmas miracle.

brigitte

Brigitte and I are keeping company. Considering that she is a four month-old beagle puppy the nature of our courtship is predictable: I court her cooperation and she courts my approbation. I am trying to housebreak her, and she is trying to figure out why I laugh and smile at her one minute and stamp my foot the next.

Brigitte is an appealing puppy, as most are. Her black, brown and white body is still small enough to be held, and her brown ears feel like velvet to the cheek. Her face, framed by the fluid ears, is expressive. When she is sleepy or beseeching affection the ears hang slack and the eyes are gentle. When she has done something wrong and knows it her eyes are evasive and her lidless brows, spiked with two or three black hairs, wink and twitch as the brown eyes look everywhere except at me. When she is full of deviltry and fun she races madly around the house and then flops on her small haunches, propping herself on sturdy front paws, one ear flipped back over her head so that she looks breathless and windblown. Sometimes she has trouble controlling her soft upper lip and it gets caught up in her teeth. When this happens her expression, as she looks up, alert, with the lip folded up into her mouth, is foolish.

Brigitte was a birthday gift for Jamie so she is called "Jamie's Dog." By choice she is Leslie's dog, for she prefers Leslie's ear-rubbing ministrations to those of any other member of the family. In *fact* she is my dog because most of her time is spent with me and it is at my hands that she is learning her lessons.

Brigitte has a lot to learn. I am most anxious to housebreak her, but there are other lessons I must teach her. She must learn that her food doesn't really taste better when she carries it from her dish to the dining room rug. She must learn that the night is long and just because she wakes refreshed at 1:30 a.m. she cannot leave her bed. She must learn that she cannot chew the magazine that came in today's mail or one of yesterday's socks that she has found on the bedroom floor. And she must learn not to plague the three cats. (This lesson the cats will teach her and because they, in their age, are not very patient she will learn it quickly.)

I despair at times about the toilet training, but I have hope, for Brigitte has shown me that she is capable of learning: she is learning about The Chair. She picked out one chair in the front room that she considered hers. I have had to chase her out of it a dozen times a day, but at last she begins to understand that she doesn't belong in it. Now when I find her there she vacates it in a rush and takes refuge behind the couch to sleep beside the warm radiator. But there are times when she makes a game out of this discipline. If our relationship seems happy to her she will rush before me into the room and jump into The Chair and sit, ear flipped onto her head, lip caught up in her teeth, and look at me as if to say, "Go ahead, tell me."

"Brigitte," I say sternly. "Get down." She wiggles and barks and waits until I take a step toward her before she jumps down to run with glee out of my reach. She seems to know when my mood is right for such play.

Brigitte and I devote most of our time together to learning everyday lessons, but we have been through crisis together too. The work on the new addition at the back of the house is underway. The cellar hole has been dug, and the foundation poured. This has been floored over, but a trench a foot or more in width and the depth of a room remains between the foundation and solid ground. Eventually this will be filled in, but right now it is a moat of sorts holding a foot of icy, muddy water.

The other afternoon, when the rest of the family was away from home, I went out on the platform to call Brigitte in. She came to the far side of the platform where there is no walkway laid across the moat.

"Come on," I urged, expecting her to come around to the other side. Brigitte is learning to come when called, and she wanted to get into the house for her supper. She stepped across the moat with her front paws and reached tentatively forward for firm footing with one short hind leg. Even as I leaned down to help, her clumsy feet slipped, and I stood with open mouth and saw her fall ... almost it seemed in slow motion ... down, down, down into the moat. Splash! She landed spread-eagle in the cold, slushy water.

I moved quickly, dramatic notions of survival time in icy water running through my mind. I ran into the house, pulled on high boots and grabbed a towel from the kitchen. Luckily a ladder lay in the yard, and as I dragged it to the edge of the moat I called to the whimpering dog, "I'm coming. I'm coming, Brigitte." I lowered the heavy ladder into the deep but narrow trench. Draping the towel over my shoulder, I started down, apprehensive as under my weight the mud and water sucked the ladder in.

At the bottom the water came within a quarter of an inch of the top of my boots. I inched along the cold concrete wall toward the feebly floundering puppy, calling encouragement as I went. When I reached her and picked her up out of the muddy water her front paws dog paddled the air, and where I held her it seemed that her heart was beating in my hand. Poor Brigitte! She whimpered and groaned. "There, there. It's all right. I've got you. It's going to be all right." I wrapped her in the towel and up we went. I was thankful she was a little dog, for how would I have hoisted a big one out of that moat?

In the house I ran warm water in the tub and sponged Brigitte off. I took her to sit beside the warm bathroom radiator while I rubbed her down, wondering if she trembled with cold or fright. Of course it was both. She had warm milk in the kitchen and by the time evening fell I was chasing her out of The Chair, although perhaps reluctantly.

the flu

The three children are sick, and the cats are happy. They like finding warm bodies in bed during the day. Hero likes to be on Stephanie's bed. She sits just out of reach, and Stephanie talks to her. Hero prefers such attention to being patted. But Eve stays in Leslie's room. She snuggles close and turns her orange tummy up to be scratched. Leslie, as sick as she feels, obliges. Adam comes in out of the cold and visits each sick room, climbing at last onto Leslie's bed where feverish Leslie finds it comforting to stroke his cold fur.

Brigitte enjoys our flu ridden household too. She likes finding food in the bedrooms. This afternoon she stole Jamie's toast and even made off with his Aspergum, which had been laid aside in favor of a cup of soup.

I don't agree with the animals. Three warm, indeed feverish, bodies mean more than just companionship for me. I take temperatures, serve juice and soup, dispense aspirin, enforce gargling, read stories and smooth rumpled beds. But I am coping very well, partly because our crises have been staggered.

Jamie started us off on Wednesday morning with fever, nausea, and chills. That afternoon the girls came home from school feeling sore and headachy and were glad to get into bed.

Thursday all three felt sick enough to be in bed, and I made the rounds with the thermometer, aspirin, juice, towel and wash cloth, and my best talcum powder. Jamie was feeling better even though he still had a slight fever. He was in bed with his Hot Wheels cars, Winnie-the-Pooh, some puzzles, six books, a set of cowboys and Indians, his drumsticks and the slab of wood he drums on, and Brigitte.He got up to wash and put on fresh pajamas while I shooed the dog, smoothed the bed, and put a clean case on the pillow. When he was settled again with an extra pillow behind his back, with Brigitte waiting nearby for me to leave so she could get back on the bed, Jamie said, "We need a mother when we are sick."

I went on to Stephanie. Her fever was not very high, but her eyes looked sick and she was content to lie flat and still. After doing what I could to make her comfortable I tucked her in and said, "Oh, Steph, I'd like to be ten years old again having my mother take care of me because I had the flu."

Partly I said that because Stephanie's blue and white room and the old spool bed with its Martha Washington spread and patchwork quilt looked so inviting, but mostly I said it because I remember what it was like to lay sick in bed while my mother worked nearby. I felt secure, sheltered from the world. And there was strange luxury in being in bed in the middle of the morning, legitimately released from the responsibility of going to school. I remember too the sense of unreality, of being out of myself, that went with a fever: the lights behind the eyes, the ringing voice that repeated some word over and over again in my head, the way my mind's eye traced some geometric pattern. These were not unpleasant sensations.

I moved on to Leslie's room. I washed her hands and face, gently rubbing away the peace sign she had inked onto her palm.

"It feels funny having someone do things for you," said Leslie, who will soon be twelve.

"These things must be done for us when we're very young, when we're sick, and when we get very old," I said. How hard it must be, I thought, to be old and still free in spirit and mind, but trapped by an infirm body.

Stephanie's fever went up during the day, and she felt progressively worse. Early in the evening her crisis came. She brought up the juice and aspirin she'd just taken. When she was back in bed, her face white as paper, unnatural bright spots on each cheek she said triumphantly, *"There,* I feel better!"

That evening Bob had a dinner meeting. I was glad not to have to cook. After settling the children for the night, I curled up on the couch with a book. I was tired. An hour or so later Jamie's crisis came. I heard strange noises coming from his room and hurried upstairs. He was sitting up in bed, tears running down his cheeks.

"I can't breathe," he gasped.

Jamie had the croup. He clambered out of bed and stood gasping for breath, stamping his feet. We'd been through croup before, but it had never seemed this bad. I felt panicky and tried to remember just how serious croup can be. I wished that Bob were home.

"I can't breathe," squeeked Jamie. "I'm going to die." That snapped me out of *my* panic.

"Oh no you're not," I said stoutly, and rushed to get the vaporizer. Within ten minutes Jamie sat beside it with his head under a towel that I'd draped over it tent fashion.

"It's steamy under here," he said.

"Good. That's what we want. Breathe deeply."

It didn't take him long to feel better and bringing his head out from under the towel he said, "We could set up my pup tent." By the time Bob walked in Jamie was ready to agree that he did indeed sound like a trained seal when he coughed. Later when we put him back to bed he said to no one in particular, "I just don't know what I'd do without a mother."

The next morning the doctor came, and today we are definitely on the mend. Even Leslie, who is still content to be in bed, feels somewhat better. Jamie and Stephanie have normal temperatures again, and there are other signs that tell me they'll soon be going back to school. I had to take away the bell I'd given Jamie when his croup turned into laryngitis: ringing it had become his favorite diversion. He and Stephanie don't want to stay in bed any more and when Jamie gets up he stares out of the window at the snow fort he built in the yard.

I stare out of the window too and think about all the households in town who are battling the flu. This is part of the winter season and because of it and the bitter cold weather and the blizzards we haven't had yet, we'll have earned spring when it comes.

errol flynn

Thanks to Errol Flynn I didn't get my work done this morning. By 9:30 I'd made a start on various projects and was about to start the ironing when I decided I'd better see what the children, who are home on vacation, were doing. I was afraid they were watching television. They were.

"Turn it off," I said from the doorway. "Leslie, get your room vacuumed. Jamie, I want the back porch picked up. Stephanie, you must have something that needs doing in your room." The only one who heard me was Stephanie, and she said, "Oh, please, Mama. This is good!"

"What are you watching anyway?" I asked, stepping into the room to see for myself. And there on the screen was Errol Flynn: mustache, cleft chin, bedroom eyes, and all. Handsome devil! "Oh, for heaven's sake! Errol Flynn!" I said. "I haven't seen one of his movies for years."

"Oh, please, Mama," Stephanie begged. "Let us watch it."

(Errol Flynn was talking to a homely lady who was obviously Queen Elizabeth. Or rather she was talking to him. "Well, Captain Thorpe, have you had a successful mission?"

"Yes, indeed, Your Grace." He handed her a rolled parchment. "Here is the inventory of our plunder, a rich take as you can see, and Your Majesty free to state her share of it."

"Splendid," said the Queen as she scanned the list.

"Your Grace, if you are pleased, may I ask a favor?"

"What is it you wish?"

"The Armada . . . may I give the Sea Hawks the order to prepare to meet the Armada?" The Queen threw the parchment down upon the table and snapped angrily, "The Armada! Is that all I'm to hear? England will win this contest with the Spanish through the art of diplomacy and not by fighting at sea. Besides, what makes you think Philip will attack England?"

"What makes you think he will not?" countered Captain Thorpe boldly.)

"Oh, dear," I said, sinking onto the couch. "Why do they put these movies on in the morning when I don't have time to watch?"

"The Sea Hawks," said Leslie. "That's what it's called."

"I used to love these movies," I said. "Good old fashioned swashbucklers."

"What's a swashbuckler?" Jamie asked.

"That!" I replied, pointing to Captain Thorpe who was now back at sea standing on the deck of his ship, long hair curling at the open collar of his shirt, eyes scanning the horizon, hand resting lightly on the hilt of the sword that hung at his side, ready for trouble.

(Trouble came. The captain and his men were captured by the Spanish and dragged before a hooded magistrate of the Spanish court. The judge read a long list of grievances against Thorpe and his men.

"How do you plead?" he intoned ominously. Captain Thorpe's voice was deadly calm when he answered, "The record should be changed to read twenty-one ships taken not twenty."

"So be it," said the judge. "You and your men are hereby sentenced to hard labor as galley slaves for the rest of your lives.")

Ah, doom! A fate worse than death, and everyone knows there is no escaping from the galley. But the movie was only half over.

"Don't worry," I reassured the children. "They'll get away."

(Meanwhile back at the court of Queen Elizabeth a lovely maiden was strumming a lute and serenading the Queen and her ladies. As she finished a messenger strode into the room.

"Pardon, Your Majesty, but word has just been received that Captain Thorpe has been seized by the Spanish and condemned to hard labor as a galley slave." The lovely maiden swooned.)

"She must love Thorpe," I said. Not having seen the beginning of the movie I had to figure out who was who as the action moved along. But that wasn't difficult for me; I'd seen too many Errol Flynn-Cornel Wilde-Paul Henreid movies in my time not to be able to figure out the plot of this one.

(Although shocked by Thorpe's capture the Queen still couldn't bring herself to arm the Sea Hawks against an armada she didn't believe existed. To make matters worse she was persuaded by one Lord Wolvington to confiscate the ships of the Sea Hawks so that they would not contribute more incidents to the strained relations between Spain and England. Anyone could see that the Sea Hawks, although privateers, were England's greatest hope against the Spanish!)

"I don't like that Wolvington," I said. "He looks like a snake in the grass to me."

(Meanwhile back on the Spanish ship Captain Thorpe was down but not out. He had learned that the Armada was about ready to sail against England and that secret letters from King Philip to his spies at Elizabeth's court were even now on board and waiting to be sent to England. Thorpe wanted desperately to get free, secure this tangible proof of the Armada's existence, and sail for England to present the proof to the Queen. And that's just what he did.)

We watched spellbound as the Englishmen struggled to get free of their chains.

"They'll use those chains to overpower the guards," I speculated out loud. They did.

"Don't tell, Mama," Stephanie admonished me.

(The guards were overcome, the ship taken, the papers secured, and Thorpe strode the deck of the ship crying, "Free the mainsail. We're for England." The background music swelled.)

"Hurrah!" I cried. The children stared at me in mild surprise.

(Once safely in England Thorpe set out for the palace to deliver the papers to Elizabeth. On the way there he met his lady love (the girl who had swooned), and she tearfully confessed that she loved him.

"I've loved you since I first saw you in the rose garden," she said. Thorpe professed himself speechless with joy which was just as well because he'd been recognized by the Spanish ambassador who ordered his guards to seize Thorpe. There seemed to be quite a lot of Spanish guards at the English court, but Thorpe managed to get inside the palace. Of course once inside he met Lord Wolvington who was after all King Philip's spy at Elizabeth's court.)

"The Villain. I knew it," I said with satisfaction.

(Thorpe and Wolvington had a spectacular sword fight in the antechamber to the Queen's apartments. Jamie and I enjoyed the sword play. Thorpe ran Wolvington through, but was immediately set upon by four guards (English I assume) who did not know that Wolvington was the villain. It appeared that all was lost, for as gallant a fighter as Thorpe was, he was spent from his duel with Wolvington and no match for four fresh swordsmen. And that was when Thorpe's lady love appeared with Queen Elizabeth in tow.

"Stop, I command you," cried Elizabeth. Thorpe sank wearily to his knee before her, and reaching into his doublet managed to pull forth the packet he carried there.

"Your Majesty. Secret documents to Wolvington telling of the sailing of the Armada.")

"Is that all? I hope that isn't all," said Stephanie.

(The final scene showed Thorpe being knighted by Elizabeth while his lady love, his crew, the Sea Hawks, the Queen's guards, the Queen's lords and advisors (minus Wolvington), and her ladies-in-waiting stood by and watched.)

"And they went on to defeat the Armada," I concluded. "Now turn it off. Leslie, go vacuum your room. Jamie, clean up the porch. Stephanie, come help me. The morning's gone, and I have hardly begun my work, thanks to Errol Flynn!"

the elephant rock

Easter will always be the Elephant Rock and losing a new overshoe and my mother's voice floating up out of the woods. It must have happened the year that I was four. Easter was coming, for Mama had started to save egg shells for us to color. When she used an egg in her cooking she made a small hole in each end of it and blew its contents into a bowl, leaving the shells whole for us children to color on the Saturday before Easter. The ritual would serve no purpose except to delight us and to mark Easter's coming.

On a sunny morning about a week before Easter Mama sent us out to play. I wore my new overshoes and was committed to the care of Joan and John. I remember that Charlie Goodrich came by, and we sat on the back steps feeling the warm sun on our hands and the cold spring air on our faces. The matted, yellow grass in the yard and the mud which oozed around the edges of the sidewalk made the prospects for play seem slight and perhaps it was that raw landscape plus the view across the long back field to the black woods that made the older children think of the Elephant Rock.

"Say." (Perhaps it was John who spoke.) "Let's go out to the Elephant Rock." The Rock was a massive grey outcropping that rose in the center of the woods, dwarfing tall pine trees, its eminence and isolation in the woods stirring the imagination to chilling games of Indians or bandits. I had never been to the

Elephant Rock, and it loomed large in my imagination as a frightening but desirable place.

"Will she have to come?" asked Charlie, gesturing toward me.

"Yes. Mama said we've got to watch her."

"She'll spoil everything if she comes. And how'll she get up the rock?"

"We'll get her up. John can bring his rope." I listened with fascination and dread to this discussion of the problem of my company, and when we set out across the field I hung behind looking back now and then to our small white house, feeling a sense of growing insecurity as it receded further and further away. The older children waited impatiently for me at the edge of the woods calling, "Hurry up, slow poke." And even as I hurried to catch up I wished Mama would appear at the distant back door and call us back.

In the woods we threaded our way around the debris winter had left — fallen branches and lingering snow patches. Where the snow had gone the ground was spongy and at one point we forded a brook swollen with spring water. It made a running music, but my pleasure in the sound was overshadowed by my tension at having to cross a bridge of logs that the boys had enthusiastically thrown down. We saw pussy willows, but it was too early for Mayflowers or bunchberry.

Our path to the Elephant Rock was desultory, its location not exactly known by the older children, but John and Charlie went ahead as scouts, and at last Joan and I heard John's Tarzan-like call and looked up to see him away and above us, visible through a gap in the closely aligned trees. We reached the Rock and from the ground its grey mass bulged upward. The rope must have been needed to help me up.

The summit of the Rock undulated. Here and there pockets held puddles of cold water. Juniper had managed to sprout in a crevice and grew in a spiney clump. Many of the trees which grew up close to the sides of the rock had reached their maximum height at its summit, but a few ancient pines had surpassed even the height of the rock, and these trees had dropped old cones onto its surface. The wind busied itself in the tips of the pines and eddied on the flat open expanse of the rock and then swept off into the woods, its sweep accentuating one's sense of delicious danger or insecurity — whatever one's viewpoint happened to be.

John loved the danger of it and wished for an advancing army to be held off from the fortress-like pinnacle. I was told to stay away from the edge and didn't need to be told. I had already sat down, glad of the solid rock despite its penetrating cold.

Joan, John, and Charlie decided that they were pioneers and that Indians were attacking from the woods, sending arrows raining onto the rock. I decided that I wanted to go home.

"I want to go home."

"Here are some nice pine cones. See, you can build something with them."

Joan was flat on her stomach behind the juniper bush and John and Charlie were defending her with rifle shots at the Indians, who had scaled some of the tall pine trees, when I dared to ask again.

"I want to go home."

"Dumb kid. I knew she'd spoil our fun."

"Don't you want to play with the pine cones?" asked Joan.

"I'm hungry," I said.

"We haven't got anything to eat, but I'll tell you what . . . how'd you like to put your feet in the puddles? Wouldn't that be nice?" I watched mutely as the new overshoes came off and then my shoes and stockings. I was led to the largest puddle and perhaps it was the shock of the cold water that made me realize what it was I really wanted.

"I want Mama," I wailed.

The Indian fighters came and stood over me.

"I told you we shouldn't have brought her."

"Baby!"

"I want Mama. I want to go home."

"Why don't you take her home and then come back," John said to Joan. "You could bring some crackers and peanut butter with you."

"You've got to come too," said Joan.

"I'm cold," I cried.

"Aw, there's no sense in staying here. She's spoiled all our fun." The imaginary Indians had fled in the face of my demands.

"We'd better go home." I stopped crying, and Joan was pulling on my socks when we heard Mama calling.

"Jo-anne. John." The wind stretched the words and floated them up to us. I must have been the only one to feel relief and probably cried all over again with the release of it.

"Gee, it's Mama, and I'll bet she's mad."

"Jo-anne. John. Where are you?"

"Up here," called John. "On the Elephant Rock." She appeared below us, and she was carrying a switch.

"What are you doing up there? Where's Joyce? What do you mean bringing that baby out here? You come down here this minute."

I don't remember coming off the rock. I do remember that one of my new overshoes could not be found, which was unfortunate, for it compounded Mama's anger. I don't remember getting home through the woods, but I do remember being put to bed in the bedroom off the kitchen (the three of us in one bed) and Mama taking out her anger on the Easter eggs which she smashed and threw away. As a parent I have experienced that kind of anger, born of fear for the safety of my children and frustration with their unconcern for some material thing whose acquisition required careful budgeting. I lay in the bed between my brother and sister; warm, secure again, glad to be back in my mother's care, tracing with my eye the scrolled border of the flowered wallpaper from corner to corner of the room. I was content.

Later, while the sun was still high, we were allowed to get up. We were dressed in clean clothes and were put this time into the front yard. Joan and John sang and danced about on the sidewalk, happy to be out of bed and in the sun of spring and done with their punishment. I was puzzled by their high spirits and said, "Mama broke all the Easter eggs."

"That's okay," was the reply. "She'll make some more." And she did.

durrell's bridge

Our Bridge — Durrell's Bridge — which spans the river just beyond our house, is made of steel and concrete, with bright orange underpinnings and smooth silver railings. Its approaches are gentle, and the road bed is wide and moves in an unbroken line of macadam over the river. It is a utilitarian, safe bridge, a model of modern planning and execution, a tribute to the men who worked two (or was it three) springtimes ago to build it. But I wish it was an old fashioned, covered bridge. I wish it was made of wood and not too wide, with a gently arched portal and a shingled roof. I wish I could look out of my window and see its barn-like structure stamped against the landscape of the old river bank and the cow pasture beyond.

My sentiments are, I realize, just that — sentiment. When the funds for the present bridge were voted at town meeting, I thought about a covered bridge, but I kept my thoughts to myself. Imagine the reaction of the town fathers to such a proposal. They were thankful to be able to look forward at last to being rid of the constant repair and upkeep of the old wooden bridge. I don't think they would have placed much stock in the argument that was put forward once by a farmer who explained that bridges were covered for the same reason that women wore petticoats — "to protect their underpinnings."

And then too the decision for this bridge did not come just from Kennebunk's selectmen and voters, for Durrell's Bridge is half in Kennebunk and half in Arundel. If the towns had indeed considered whether to have a covered bridge or a concrete bridge we might have ended up with the kind of bridge that was built years ago by the towns of Buxton and Hollis. The two towns couldn't agree on whether to build with wood or iron, so Buxton built her half of the bridge of iron and Hollis built her half of wood.

The State Highway Commission would not have considered building a covered bridge on our well travelled road either. Their safety experts would have had a lot to say about the dangers of the confining approaches and portals. And they would have been right. Often in the evening when we are sitting in our front room, or at night when we are in bed, and sometimes during the daylight hours, we hear the roar of a speeding car whose driver is testing himself and his car to see how fast he can take the sweep onto the bridge. I'm afraid a barn-like entrance would not deter such drivers from their game, but would only serve as more of a challenge to them. There is no doubt that not every speeder would make his pass successfully. It wouldn't have done any good either to put up a sign (as was done on the portal of a covered bridge in Taftsville, Vermont, once-upon-a-time) warning: "One dollar fine for a person to drive a horse or beast faster than a walk on this bridge."

Historically there is no justification for Durrell's Bridge to be covered. There were shipyards on our river bank years ago, and the ships were floated down river from this site to Kennebunkport where they were fitted with masts. In those days Durrell's Bridge was a draw so that it could be raised to let them through.

But covered bridges did used to be common in Maine (which had 120 of them at one time) because our state had a surplus of lumber and skilled shipwrights. So perhaps raising a covered bridge on our road today could have been excused on the basis that it was a memorial to the shipwrights who worked at Kennebunk Landing over a hundred years ago.

Shipbuilding is not a common occupation today, and it would have been a challenge to find carpenters who would have been willing and able to build such a bridge. But what pleasure we would have had in strolling down to watch them raising a Burr Truss or a Town Lattice Truss. The sights and sounds of such activity would have been more pleasant than the workings of the great, yellow diesel-powered dozers and cranes that labored here to build the present bridge.

Arguments against building a covered bridge would not have been hard to find, but I can think of as many gentle reasons why such a bridge would have been justified. People would have enjoyed it — tourists, camera buffs, artists. And think of the children who would have begged to be driven through the "bridge with a roof." We might, like our ancestors, have called it a wishing bridge, making a wish each time we passed through it. Or it might have been called a kissing bridge! In time the children might have conjured up a ghost for it and hopefully it would have been a ghost who would haunt the passersby who throw their beer cans and Dairy Queen papers along our road.

Those of us who live on Durrell's Bridge Road would have taken pleasure in walking down to the bridge, coming into its cool shelter on hot summer days, seeing the shimmer of the water on its beams and hearing the chatter of barn swallows who might have chosen to build in its rafters. We might have run to shelter in it when a sudden shower caught us unaware, and we would have savored the feeling of secretiveness that would have come to us under its roof in sun or shower or at twilight. Our voices and footsteps would have echoed a little in its tunnel. And we might have woken in the night to hear the muffled rumble of cars that slowed to maneuver its length.

A covered bridge would have slowed us all in our headlong race to come and go and be. If our present bridge stands as a monument to progress, a covered bridge might have stood as a reminder of our human need for something besides speed and efficiency.

paradise

"Come to Maine with us," our Uncle Bob said to his friend Lloyd. "Mary and I are going down to my sister's for a week and she said they can put up three of us if you'd like to come along. There are two or three golf courses in the area and beautiful beaches, and we'll have some fried clams and lobster."

"Sounds like Paradise," said Lloyd, and so he locked the door on his bachelor apartment and headed for Maine with Uncle Bob and Aunt Mary.

They drove down from The City. Somewhere in Massachusetts a crashing hailstorm caught them by surprise, shattering a window in Lloyd's car. If this seemed an omen that even Paradise might not be perfect, they were reassured at the entrance to the Maine Turnpike where they were greeted by clear skies, the clean smell of pine, and a friendly attendant at the toll booth. Maine, it seemed, could offer nothing but good weather, friendly people, clean living, and rest and relaxation.

("... some sigh for the prophet's Paradise to come ...")*

Here in Paradise we were ready for them, having spent the day in frenzied preparation. When they arrived late in the evening the house was peaceful. The three children were asleep on cots in a back room, the dog had gone to her bed in the shop, and the cats had been put out for the night.

("... now sing recover'd Paradise ...")

In the rooms the children had vacated for our guests we had put vases of flowers on bedside tables, and the windows were open to the sweet night air. The open windows also admitted the sounds of the night, and I wondered if the cacophony of the peepers in the river marsh beyond the house might not be too loud for city dwellers who are only used to the sounds of traffic.

"Perhaps that's too noisy for you," I said to Lloyd as he stood

---

*This and all other Paradise quotes are from *Dictionary of Quotations*, collected and arranged and with comments by Bergen Evans, Delacorte Press, 1968.

surveying the toy trucks, cowboy hats, and stuffed animals that furnished the room that was to be his.

"Yes," he agreed. "Let me take this slowly." Even Paradise takes some getting used to.

Our children are early risers and knowing that there is company in the house is added incentive to GET UP. We tried to be quiet and were, I think, fairly successful except for our comings and goings in the bathroom which is accessible from two doorways, one of which opens out of the upstairs hallway bordering on Lloyd's room while the other leads directly into the bedroom we had given to Mary and Bob. We were eating breakfast when Uncle Bob appeared in the kitchen, unwashed and unshaven. I thought perhaps the smell of freshly perked coffee had drawn him downstairs, but it seems that someone had left the bathroom door leading to his room locked. "You locked me out," he said as he kept right on going through the kitchen and up the back stairs to the back hallway and the other bathroom door.

"I'm glad that didn't happen to Lloyd," I said. At least Uncle Bob was family.

Lloyd was up early too, but the aroma of coffee didn't bring him down either, for it turned out that he liked tea for breakfast.

"How did you sleep?" we asked.

"Fine. Just great. I went right to sleep and slept soundly till 6 a.m., but then I kept hearing bells ringing."

"Bells? Oh yes, that would be the cats. They all wear bells so they won't catch birds." The cats, beginning at dawn, pace in the yard below the bedroom windows, wanting to come into the house for breakfast.

"How many cats do you have?" asked Lloyd.

"Three." Later in the day I divested the cats of their bells.

It was a beautiful day and everyone went off in a different direction to do something different. Our guests drove off to tour the beaches and to do a little shopping in the town. They very kindly took the children with them and when they returned Jamie came into the house carrying a large box of strawberries.

"Lloyd bought us some strawberries," he said. It was a generous gift, for strawberries, being out of season, were expensive. We thanked Lloyd, but he said it was Jamie who deserved our thanks. In the store Jamie had followed him around, and when asked conversationally, "What do we need?" Jamie had answered hopefully, "They've got some nice strawberries."

"Hmmm. Yes," said Lloyd, noting the price. "Maybe we'd better get some tonic."

"Well," said Jamie. "Maybe we'd better get some strawberries."

"Do you like strawberries, Jamie?"

"Oh, yes. And my mother likes strawberries, and my father likes strawberries, and my sister Leslie likes strawberries, and my sister Stephanie likes strawberries, and Uncle Bob likes strawberries and ..."

"Okay, okay," said Lloyd. "We'll get some strawberries."

("... he on honey dew hath fed,
And drunk the milk of Paradise ...")

After that Jamie counted Lloyd his particular friend and during the course of the day invited him to share his ball and bat, his basketball, and his bicycle. At five o'clock when we gathered for cool drinks before dinner Jamie and Lloyd were not to be found. At last an exhilarated Jamie and a somewhat subdued Lloyd appeared coming up the drive.

"We went for a walk in the woods," said Jamie.

"Walk!" exclaimed Lloyd. "We've been MILES into the woods. He kept going and going, wanting to show me this and show me that. We fished for polywogs in the pond and played hide and seek in the woods and hunted for animal tracks. That's quite a boy you've got there." He collapsed into a chair, ready for a tall, cold drink.

("... and thou beside me in the wilderness
Oh, wilderness were Paradise enow ...")

It had been a long day for all of us, and that evening we sat in front of a cheerful fire recouping our lost energies. That was the night the Kelleys arrived: Uncle John, Aunt Georgaline, Kathleen, Nancy, and the dog, Cocoa.

"What a nice surprise," I cried.

"Well, we had a free week, and just thought we'd drive to Maine," explained John. We made room for them in front of the fire, and everyone talked at once, and Lloyd sat in a corner, his face a study in friendly and apologetic bewilderment.

("Today shalt thou be with me in Paradise.")

The arrival of the Kelleys did not present sleeping problems because they had brought their camper with them, but the bathroom was busy in the morning and breakfast was a production. Lloyd was seventh in line for the bathroom and perhaps it was he who left the door to Uncle Bob's room locked on that morning, for as Lloyd stood in the kitchen saying, "Let me cook the bacon; I'm a very skillful cooker of bacon," Uncle Bob came through mumbling, "Locked out again."

("Domestic happiness, thou only bliss
Of Paradise that has survived the fall.")

During the days that followed there was golf, trips to the beach, fishing, fried clams, and rain. On one rainy day I took the children to visit the library and thirteen year old Kathleen brought home three books on witches. When Lloyd, who teaches literature, commented on her choice of reading material she explained seriously, "I'm very interested in the black arts."

During another rainy interval the children painted pictures with melted crayons, and when the dog inadvertantly upended the containers of melted wax onto a braided rug we took a picture Nancy had painted and hung it in a prominent place. It was a picture of a large black dot and around it she had written in bright letters, "Panic Button. Push."

We had music too, for three of the young cousins take piano lessons. During one cocktail hour, while we adults were discussing the merits of school busing, Lloyd suddenly exclaimed, "Heart and Soul!"

"What's that?" I asked, and then realized that this was the name of the song the children were playing on the piano in the next room.

"It's amazing," said Lloyd, "how many different ways they can play one song."

And so it went. Lloyd came to seem like one of the family. His acceptance into our midst was symbolized by the tribute paid to him by Brigitte, who, bringing home a very large, very dead, very ripe sea gull, chose to lay it at Lloyd's feet. We took our cue from Brigitte, and when at last the week was over, and we were sharing our last meal together, we solemnly presented Lloyd with a medal (made of red, white and blue construction paper) which was inscribed:

To "Uncle" Lloyd
The seal of Kelley-Butler for
Patience and Good Humor
above and beyond what
should be called for in
Paradise

my room

My family understands me. Bob hadn't been home from work very long last night when he said, "Joyce, you're up tight."

"Yes," said Stephanie. "She's tense and irrigated."

"I think," said Bob to me, "that is a nice way of saying you're all wet."

My family understands me and a measure of their understanding is that I have a room of my own. My room opens off the back hallway, and the children call it "Mama's Writing Room." It was Virginia Woolf who said, "A woman must have a room of her own if she is to write ..."*

My room is small. It measures eight feet by eight feet. The floor is wide pumpkinpine boards, the walls are white, the woodwork is painted a rich mustardy-yellow. There is one window in my room and it looks out upon the long gardens. The window is framed by bookshelves which form a deep sill. I take pleasure in arranging treasures on the sill: a choice book, an interesting rock or shell, a seasonal bouquet. The bookshelves hold my books: novels I have enjoyed over the years, poetry, gardening books; literary criticism, the dictionary and the thesaurus I use in my writing ...

There is a desk in my room. It is an old fashioned roll-top with lots of pigeon holes, pencil trays, a secret compartment or two, and deep drawers on one side. The lamp on my desk is bronze with a teal blue shade. The surface of the desk is usually a clutter of letters to be answered, half written articles, bills to be paid, clippings to be read, lists of "Things to do today." There are treasures on my desk too: a fat mushroom that Leslie made for me in pottery class, a choice forest-green insulator, rocks that favorite children have decorated.

Above the desk hangs the painting called "The Red Chair." The

*Virginia Woolf, *A Room of One's Own,* Harcourt, Brace and World, Inc., New York, 1929

picture is of a little blue house, encroached upon by dark woods. A red chair sits in the sunlit dooryard. I value the painting because it captures the ragged, rural landscape of the Maine I know best. When I look at the picture I can almost smell warm pine and half expect to see a bent old man appear in the door of the little blue house.

My desk chair is a Windsor arm chair, old but comfortable, a treasure we salvaged from our favorite library. It sits before the desk on a small rug of multicolored braids.

The stereo is in my room, and I indulge myself with music when I write letters or do the weekly budget at the desk. And of course my typewriter is in my room, and this is where I write.

The fact that I write in my room would justify it in Virginia Woolf's eyes, and to a large degree she would be correct, for this was the main reason for setting this corner of the house aside for my use. But my room is also my haven — for reading when I want to read and the rest of the family wants to watch television, for indulging my personal taste in music, for satisfying my need for privacy and detachment from everyone. It is my special place and even when I am at home alone I enjoy being in my room.

This winter I have spent long afternoons at my desk so that when the children arrived home from school I was ready to be with them. But school is out now, and I wonder if having a room of my own will insure me the quiet moments I value? There is no door on my room and there will be much coming and going in the hallway and many young faces peering in at me wanting questions answered and problems solved. Will I be able to achieve the isolation I need to write, to read, to think, to rest?

I expressed this fear to a friend, and she brought me four "Do Not Disturb" signs, the kind that you find in a hotel room. She gave them to me half in jest, but I am going to use them. This summer when I need time alone in my room I will post one of the signs. I will tell the children that when the sign is up I am not to be disturbed unless something very important has come up.

My family understands me, and I hope their understanding will not falter when I barricade myself behind a "Do Not Disturb" sign. I rather think it will not, for I am going to give each of the children one of the signs. When Stephanie wants to play with her doll house, or Jamie wants to listen to his records, or Leslie wants to read, or when any one of them just wants time to be alone to think, to dream, to rest — he may hang his sign on his door. And the rest of us, passing by, will understand his need to be alone for a time with his treasures, his thoughts, himself.

timmy

Timmy is coming again. In a week he'll be with us. I feel as unsettled about his coming this year as I did last. Last year I felt uneasy because I did not know the child who was to spend two weeks with us; this year I am uneasy because I do know the child.

Timmy came to us through the Fresh Air Program, which originates in New York City and whose aim is to take children from the slums of the city and put them into a country environment with host families. We had heard heart-warming stories about these children: of their wonder at the beauties of nature, of their disbelief that they were actually going to sleep in a bed all alone, of the feeling of kinship that grew up between them and their "summer family." We wanted to be such a family to such a child.

We were interviewed by the program's area representative who asked if we had any preferences as to the age, sex, race or religion of our child. Our only preference was for a boy who would be close in age to Jamie.

"You will probably be assigned a Negro or Puerto Rican child," the representative said. "The program has more of these children than they can place because some areas won't take them."

On the day the Fresh Air children were to arrive we went to the town hall to wait for the bus. Many host families were there, sitting on the steps, laughing and talking, watching eagerly for sight of the bus. No one else seemed apprehensive, as I was. Doubt had grown in my mind. Were we patient enough, and did we have enough stamina to take on the care of another child? Had our children acquired prejudices we didn't know about and would they say or do anything to offend our guest? Would he be happy with us, and if problems arose would we deal with them wisely? I saw that our failures in this venture could be large.

The bus was late and when at last the word went out that it was coming the people surged down the steps to the curbing. I went with them even though my apprehension cut me off from their eagerness. The great, sleek bus, its chrome flashing in the sunlight, drew up, and behind its tinted windows I could see small, watching faces. When the children filed out some were eager and some looked as anxious as I felt. They were all Negro or Puerto Rican. I felt happy that they were welcome in our town.

One of the first to get down was an older boy who was returning, I knew, for a third or fourth visit with his family. He was beaming, and I saw his host mother waving excitedly. He bounced a little with pleasure as he went to meet her and her young children, who clung to his arm as he bent down to chuck them gently under the chin. I was surprised at the tears that came to my eyes as I watched.

I wondered which little boy was to be ours, and seeing one handsome child get off the bus thought to myself, "Oh, I'd like him to be our child." But my name was being called, and we pushed forward to meet our guest.

He was small and thin. His black hair was close cropped and his nose was flat across his face. There was dirt in the corner of one eye, and he snuffled.

"Mrs. Butler, this is Timothy Freeman." He ducked a look at me, but had no answering smile for my eager greeting.

"Hello, Timmy," I said, trying to shake his small, limp hand. "We're glad to have you with us. This is Jamie and Leslie and Stephanie." He didn't speak, and watching him I was suddenly overwhelmed at the thought of what he had faced by coming hundreds of miles away from his home to spend two weeks with complete strangers. I wondered at his courage and the courage of his mother in letting him come.

I wouldn't have been surprised if he had cried when we turned our backs on the bus, his only tie to home, but he came quietly to our car. I chattered nervously in an effort to help him make the transition. He didn't speak until on the way home Jamie complained about a loose tooth and then he said in a low voice, "Knock it out." Visions of rough, ghetto children flashed through my mind, and I felt uneasy. But when we drove into our yard Timmy cried spontaneously, "Is this it? Look at all the trees!" We were home safe.

I'd like to be able to go on to tell another of those beautiful stories about an underprivileged, black child and a white, middle-class, do-gooder family. I can't. My story is about people coming together with good intent, limited by background, facing problems in their meeting, failing — and succeeding — in their efforts to solve those problems.

Timmy and Jamie didn't get along. Their differences were

never resolved because cause and effect in their feuding were so hopelessly tangled. Which came first, Timmy's aggressive, competitive nature, or Jamie's possessiveness toward his toys, his room, and even his father? It was difficult to have Timmy come to me saying of Jamie, "He's not being nice. Why isn't he being nice?" And it was upsetting to have Jamie cry at bedtime and ask me, "When is Timmy going home?" Our only comfort was to realize that the problem was not racial. The greatest insult Jamie could hurl at Timmy was, "You dumb-dumb."

The failure of the boys to get along was only one of our preconceived notions to be shattered. Timmy was not thrilled by the excursions we planned for him. We went to the animal farm at Gray, but Timmy, who had visited the zoo in New York City, was not impressed. Fishing was not a first because he and his brothers went fishing in the city with their father. The beach did not interest him. Soon after we would arrive there he would ask to come home. Pony rides and boat rides and a visit to the trolley museum were received with little enthusiasm.

Timmy's enthusiasm was for those aspects of our life that we take for granted. He seemed to crave contact with adults, particularly with Bob.

"When is He coming home?" he would ask me again and again, and he would sit in the dirt of the driveway waiting for Bob's car to appear along the road. Timmy loved books, and they seemed an unfamiliar pleasure to him. Going to the library was something new, and he was surprised when I told him he could bring books home to read. He enjoyed music, and one of his happiest afternoons was spent watching Leslie and Stephanie performing an original play.

"It's won-nerful," he cried again and again, clapping his hands.

Timmy liked to help me in the kitchen. One day we made cookies together. I rolled out the spicy dough, and he cut out the round cookies. We saved enough dough to make six gingerbread men and agreed that these would be Timmy's suppertime surprise for the family. We carefully marked them with faces and buttons, and cooked them a golden brown. When we took them off the cookie sheet one got broken and he insisted that it be his. All of ours must be perfect.

Such were the obvious successes of our time together, modest, but more meaningful than they sound because they brought forth the eager child from behind the stoic mask he had learned to wear. Timmy must count these as happy memories too and perhaps there were others that I still do not see, because he wanted to come back this year.

Although I cannot measure what Timmy's visit here meant to him, I have come to see what having him here meant to us. We gained from his visit. We came closer to the problem of racial prejudice. We learned to fear it as black parents must. What would we do if we went into a restaurant that would not welcome Timmy or if someone called him "nigger"? These things never happened, but if they had could we have said to him, "We are so sorry" and made him feel better?

Actually instead of encountering prejudice we were startled to see how self-conscious white people have become toward blacks. Strangers would come up to us on the street and in the supermarket and smile at Timmy and pat him on the head and say, "Hello, sonny." It was as if they were saying, "Look, I'm not prejudiced." And I, at least, felt uneasy because I wondered if some of this same feeling came to me when I walked through our all white town with Timmy at my side.

Through Timmy we saw how sheltered our own children are. His tough stoicism, his self-control, his competitive struggle for place and possession were in sharp contrast to the easily ruffled feelings and soft attitudes of our own children. It was a good lesson to learn.

We could have found reasons for not inviting Timmy back this year, but it was easier to find reasons why we should. If, in the light of our difficulties, I must justify his return visit, I can only do so by saying it is important for us and for him because of what we have given each other and have yet to give.

one

"I want you to look at this," I said, interrupting Bob and the children in the middle of a television program. I held up Leslie's red, white and blue jersey. "The whites are whiter and the brights are brighter," I said.

"Oh, Mama. You sound just like a television commercial," chided Stephanie.

"I know it, but it's true, and I'm pleased."

"Joyce, are you saying that you're happy with the new soap powder you're getting from the milkman?" asked Bob.

"Laundry compound," I corrected. "It does a beautiful job besides being biodegradable."

"That means it won't pollute," said Jamie.

"That's right. It's 100 percent organic. It won't pollute because it has no phosphates and it's better for the septic tank and the plumbing because it doesn't make suds the way soap does. And I use less because it doesn't have fillers like regular detergents." (I really did sound like a commercial.) "I'm really happy about this: I feel virtuous because I'm not polluting the environment, and I'm also getting the cleanest wash I've ever had, and that's saying a lot when you consider that I wash in cold water." The family seemed properly impressed so I left them to their program and went back to my ironing.

Although I believe the responsibility for preserving our environment must be with the manufacturer, because only his reach is great enough to make a real difference, I realize too that the consumer must care. As a housewife I am the vital link between the producer and the environment. I buy the products that keep my family clean, the food we eat, the clothes we wear, and just about every product we use in our daily living. It is up to me to do what I can as an individual to stem the tide of pollution, over-consumption, wasteful packaging, and neglect that I read about in every magazine and newspaper that comes into this house.

This is why when I heard about the biodegradable laundry compound the milkman is selling I didn't hesitate to buy it, even though this left me with the problem of what to do with a just purchased, unopened box of detergent. I didn't like the thought of having spent seventy-nine cents for something I wouldn't use. Finally I got my courage up and took the detergent back to the supermarket and asked for a refund.

Now when I read an article about the corruption of Lake Erie because of an overdose of phosphates, I tell myself that I have done something to prevent such a catastrophe here.

I'm not acting alone either. Many of my friends are concerned about the pollution crisis and have taken steps to stem the tide of abuse. They too have changed to biodegradable washing products and I am not the only housewife I know who did not stock up on paper plates and cups for this summer's picnics, choosing instead to buy one inexpensive set of plastic dishes for use. . .and re-use. This means less consumption of paper goods and that means fewer trees cut down.

Now I'm worrying about newspapers. I read recently about a

new business enterprise in Chicago that collects newspapers for recycling. The papers are de-inked and reprocessed. Re-using newsprint means saving trees, something like sixteen trees per eight tons of paper. When I carry last week's *Star* and back issues of the *Monitor* out to the trash I wonder how many trees I throw away in the course of a year.

Although I am not yet doing all I can toward saving newsprint, I do return extra coat hangers to the cleaner instead of throwing them away, and I don't spray my flowers with insecticides. This last is one of the hardest decisions I've had to make. My peonies have a blight. I have a spray I know will cure them, but I haven't used it. It sits on a high shelf in the shed (because I don't know how to dispose of it safely), and the leaves on my peonies curl and blacken and some of the buds this year were brown and hard.

The problem of insecticides is one of the gravest in the pollution story, and in this area I feel very unsure of myself. What do I know about carbaryl, dimethyl, trichiorcethanol; names from the label of the spray I am not using on my peonies? What does it mean when the label says "contains spreader" and "systematic action?" I don't know, but I do understand what it means when it says, "Warning: This product is toxic to fish and wildlife.Keep out of lakes, ponds and streams." And robins, I might add.

There is much to be done to save our environment. We each do what we can, and wonder what our efforts amount to. I don't know the answer to that either. But I think of the words I saw on a poster once:

> What can I do
> towards a better
> world? I am one . . .
> I am only one. . .
> but I am one.

the pond

We went to the pond: Stephanie, Jamie and I. The supper dishes were cleared away, Leslie was at a friend's house, Bob was at work, and the evening hours stretching before us seemed to call for some special pastime.

"Let's take a bicycle ride," I said. Our intent was to bicycle along the River Road, but it was predictable that we would end up at the pond.

The evening air, blowing on our faces as we coasted down the road and across the bridge that spans our tidal river, smelled of the heat of the day. It smelled too of the green and growing countryside, of wild roses, and, faintly, of fresh water. And so I thought of the pond. When we turned along the River Road I looked across the pasture field to the row of pine trees that grow along its edge.

"Let's stop at the pond," I called to Stephanie and Jamie.

"Okay," cried Jamie. "Follow me." And we did, although we knew the way.

We left our bicycles at the pasture gate and climbed through the bars. There weren't any cows in the field. They were in the barn being milked. We pushed our way through the field, knee-deep in clover.

"See how lovely the clover is," I said. I traced the stem of a particularly lush blossom down into the tangle of vetch, daisies, and buttercups, and snapped the blossom free. "Let's take a bouquet home." Picking slowed our progress to the pond, but we talked.

"When your Grammy and Grampa B. were married years ago in a little country church they decorated the church with huge bouquets of wild clover."

"Why?" asked Jamie.

"Because clover is beautiful, and there was lots of it. Like this. Here, just smell these flowers." I held up the bouquet of fat, pink globes and the children dutifully bent their faces over it.

"Smell mine," said Stephanie, who had been picking daisies and yellow buttercups.

"Daisies are pretty to see, Stephanie, but they don't smell very good."

"I'd like to be married in a field," said Jamie, who had been thinking about the church decorated with clover.

"Yes," I nodded. "There are young people today who choose to be married out of doors . . .near the ocean, on a mountain . ."

"Why?"

"Because they think love comes from God," I said, not defining God. "And this is God's world."

"Do you think that?"

"Yes."

"Look, Mama. Isn't the pond beautiful," said Stephanie. We had come through the line of trees. The pond *was* beautiful: serene, a separate place enclosed by evening bird song and the forest against which it drew its gentle arc away and beyond. A wood duck flew up against the late blue sky; otherwise there was no movement there except our own and the busy tracery of water striders on the surface of the water.

"We can catch a frog," suggested Stephanie. "You come up behind them and catch them and hold them by their legs to look at them and then you let them go."

"I'm glad you let them go," I said.

"There's one," cried Jamie. I looked to see a frog in the shallow, grassy water at the edge of the pond. He was submerged except for the top of his bright lemony-green head and round, black, yellow-ringed eyes. I scootched down and spoke to him.

"Hello there. Aren't you handsome. Do you eat those water striders for your supper?" The black eyes regarded me brightly. "Talk to me," I said.

"They croak when you hold them," Stephanie explained.

"I *would* like to hear him talk."

"They have bright yellow stomachs too," she added.

"I *would* like to see that."

"I'll catch him," said Jamie.

"Be gentle," I urged. Jamie reached for the frog who jumped handily away and sat just out of reach watching us calmly. "He's not afraid is he. Wouldn't you think he'd swim away."

"There's another one." There were frogs all along the edge of the pond: sleek, amphibious Buddhas. But we lost interest in the frogs when we found the deer track. It was incised in the wet earth at the edge of the water. A deer had come to drink at some dawn or evening time.

"I'm going to sit down for a bit before we head back," I told the children. My bouquet was drooping, so I laid the stems in the edge of the water and sat down nearby. Jamie came to stand near me.

"I'd like to go wading," he announced.

"Go ahead."

"Oh boy! Steph let's go wading." They left their sneakers on the grass and stepped gingerly into the soft mud. Jamie hiked his dungarees up as high as they would go, which wasn't very high. It was inevitable that they were soon a little wet. He stood in the water holding up his pant legs. "I'd like to go swimming," he said.

"Go ahead," I said again.

"Really? In my clothes?"

"Why not." He chuckled and turning dove head first into the water. He came up grinning and exclaiming, "Beautiful! It's beautiful!" It took Stephanie a little longer to get in.

"Oh, I'm standing in mud up to my ankles," she fussed. "I guess I'll come out." But she didn't. They cavorted together, squealing and not minding the sediment that floated up from the riled bottom of the pond.

At last Stephanie was cold and came out.

"It's time to go, Jamie," I said.

"This is great," he answered. Stephanie and I stood on the banking.

"Come on Jamie."

"Okay. I'm going to do a depth charge first." He held his nose and went under and came up spouting.

"Come on, Jamie."

"Okay, but first I want to try swimming without my ..." Glub, glub; he went down. "It didn't work without my kick," he said when he came up. And then he was out. "Can we come tomorrow?"

"Probably not."

"Can we come again?"

"Yes."

We waded back through the field of clover.

"Will we look funny riding our bikes home with wet clothes?"

"No one will notice." Jamie sang all the way home, fleeting along before us. Stephanie rode beside me.

"That was fun, Mama. Thanks," she said.

It was bedtime when we got home. After putting on his pajamas Jamie came to say goodnight. Bits of twigs still clung to his wet hair, and there was a sparkle in his eyes.

"I like swimming in my clothes," he said, and then after thinking a minute he added, "I don't think it's bad to swim with girls ... sometimes." And then he gave a great sigh of satisfaction and said, "You know, that was my happiest time."

a picnic

"This is the way to pack a picnic," I thought as I moved sleepily about the kitchen. It was 7 a.m., and I was making breakfast and packing a lunch to take with us on our trip to retrieve Stephanie from her stay at camp. As I took the makings of our breakfast from the refrigerator and cupboard I came across unexpected tidbits for our picnic. Opening the refrigerator to get an egg for the waffle batter, I saw a little container of Danish cheese and ham. The spread would be a tasty snack, I decided, so tucked it into the picnic basket along with a sleeve of Ritz crackers.

I had already packed hamburg patties and frankfurters and rolls for each. I had packed the mustard and relish, ketchup, a couple of hard boiled eggs, and a container of potato salad, which I'd made the night before. Thinking of the salad and knowing two of the children wouldn't eat it, I decided to make a small tossed salad too. I tossed the greens and raw vegetables together and put the dressing in a jar to be added later. I diced up the last of a wedge of cheddar cheese and put the cubes into the basket along with a handful of toothpicks to spear them. There were pickles and green olives, peaches and ginger cookies, and marshmallows to cook over the last of the charcoal fire. After breakfast I reheated the coffee I'd made that morning and filled a large thermos. I had already made lemonade for the half-gallon thermos. At last it seemed that everything was ready, but I checked to be sure I hadn't forgotten sugar for the coffee, napkins, and utensils for spooning relish, spreading cheese, scooping salad, slicing rolls, flipping hamburgers, and toasting marshmallows.

"What a picnic we're going to have," I told the children when they came to carry the basket, the cooler, and the two thermoses out to Bob who was loading the station wagon. While they helped him load the lunch and the fishing poles, my collapsible chair, a blanket, and life preservers (in case we rented a boat somewhere), I flew upstairs to get dressed.

When I came back downstairs Bob and the children were ready

to leave, but I was not. I wanted to double check to make sure we had thought of everything.

"Did you put the dog in the shop with food and water? Are all the cats out? Have you each got your bathing suits and a towel and a sweater? Do you think we should take raincoats? Are all the windows closed? Have you children made your beds? Is the iron unplugged? Has everybody been to the bathroom?"

"Is it okay to lock up now?" asked Bob, who had been standing patiently at the back door while I ran through my list.

"Oh, wait a minute. I haven't got something to read." I dashed in and found my book and then we were ready to go. As we backed out of the yard I said, "Well, I don't believe we've left anything behind."

We were forty miles from home when Bob asked casually, "By the way, how did you plan to cook the hot dogs and hamburgers?"

"The hibachi," I said, staring at him. "The hibachi and the charcoal and the lighter fluid...you didn't pack them."

"You didn't mention them."

"I forgot. I thought of them yesterday afternoon, but forgot all about them this morning."

"Well, no problem," said Bob. "Most of the state parks and picnic areas have outdoor grills, and we can pick up some charcoal and fluid at a store." I agreed, thinking of the twenty pound bag of charcoal and two cans of lighter fluid in the shed at home. "I'm sure they'll have those grills at Pemaquid." Our plan was to drive to Pemaquid Point to see the digs of that ancient settlement and Fort William Henry after picking Stephanie up at camp. We settled back, our problem solved, to enjoy the ride.

At camp, Stephanie was packed and waiting for us although I wondered if she was ready to come home, for she was casual in her greeting and seemed reluctant to leave her new friends. As far as I could discover the only thing she had missed about home was the food.

"The food was terrible here," she said, voicing that traditional childhood complaint.

"We'll make up for it at lunch," I told her. "I've packed a big picnic." We put her belongings in the station wagon and headed for Pemaquid.

"I'm hungry," said first one child and then another.

"Look, there's a nice place. Let's stop." said Leslie as we sailed past a wooded glade on the bank of a winding stream where we could see tables and grills under the trees.

"We haven't got our charcoal yet. We'll get it at the first store we come to and then stop at the next picnic spot we see if you're too hungry to wait till we get to Pemaquid." We bought some charcoal and fluid at a little store at a crossroad in the middle of everywhere, and then began in earnest our search for a place to eat. From that point on we didn't see another picnic area.

The closer we got to Pemaquid and the coast the less we saw of the sun. Fog enveloped the coast. By the time we reached the town of Pemaquid we could see very little of the white cottages ringed with gardens and picket fences that stood along the curving coast road. We were alone on the road; the fog was keeping people indoors. But weather has yet to dampen an outing for us. We were not concerned with the fog. We were concerned with finding a grill on which to cook our lunch.

"I hope there's a picnic area at the digs," I said.

We found the road to the state park and the digs. It seemed to lead out into a field. We passed, on our left, Fort William Henry, a stone tower standing in a green field with the sea just beyond.

"We'll come back," I promised the children. "Let's eat first." A gate and toll house barred our way to the digs.

"Is there a picnic area inside, with grills?" Bob asked the girl at the toll house.

"No, but there's a restaurant and a gift shop."

"Is there a picnic spot anywhere in the area that has grills?"

"Not that I know of," said the girl happily. We thanked her, said we'd be back, and turned the car around.

"What will we do?" I asked, feeling certain that we'd have to make a lunch out of all the little tidbits I'd packed instead of the hamburgers and hot dogs.

"We'll be all right if we can get down on the rocks," said Bob calmly, and looking at him I could see he had a plan.

It was Bob who thought to park the car at the fort and explore beyond the parking lot. Looking down over the shaggy grass that grew where the land dropped to the sea, we saw a small, rocky cove. The grey rocks formed a sheltered, dry bit of land before they spilled into the ocean. It was easy going down the steep embankment, and we soon had our picnic paraphenalia carried down from the car.

Bob set to work building a small fire in a pocket in the rocks.

"We can spear the hot dogs on the long handled fork," I said, "and save the hamburgers for another day."

"Just be patient," Bob told me. "We'll have hamburgers too." In no time he had found a flexible strip of rusty metal lying on the rocks. This he bent to make a grill which he laid on the leaping flames.

The rocks were our table and our chairs as well as our stove. While the meat cooked I spread out our picnic on a flat boulder, and we snacked on cheese and crackers. The air was warm there in the cove between the rocky slope and the restless sea, and while the fog didn't lift, the sun seemed to have come closer behind its curtain. A lobster boat moved just off shore. It was a dim shape in the fog, but the steady beat of its idling motor came clearly across the water.

"This is really Down East," I thought, breathing the cool, sweet scent of the sea, watching the gulls who had flown down to investigate their chances for having a share in our picnic, listening to the progress of the boat across the fog-bound inlet. I felt refreshed, comforted, released from . . . "From what?" I asked myself, and the answer was from people.

"It's really incredible," I said to Bob, "That we can be here like this at the height of the summer season with no other people around."

"I guess the fog has kept everyone home." I was thankful for the fog which gave us the chance to be alone with the sea and the gulls and the solitary fisherman on the cove. To the children I said, "Count your blessings. We are very fortunate that we can be here and not trapped in a hot city or fighting for a place on a crowded beach."

What a picnic we had. Never were there such juicy hot dogs and hamburgers, such tangy potato salad, such aromatic coffee, such succulent peaches. There was very little left to pack back into the basket. And when we had eaten there was time to hunt for sea glass among the rocks and to venture out until the surf splashed the toes of our sneakers.When it was time to leave we were careful not to leave any traces of our picnic behind. We even took away the impromptu grill upon which our meat had cooked. We left just the ashes from our fire knowing they would be scattered by the incoming tide.

We visited Fort William Henry, looking down from the tower onto the cove where we had sheltered for lunch. We went on to the digs where Leslie reminded us that some day she was going to be an archaeologist. Stephanie was as interested in a nearby graveyard as she was in the grassy depressions in the ground that marked the sites of the houses of 17th century Pemaquid. The gravestones of dead infants gave her more of a sense of the past. Bob and Jamie discovered a pier beyond the restaurant where they could fish and did, feeling satisfied even though they didn't catch a thing. I visited the gift shop where upon buying thirty-five cents worth of peppermint sticks I was given a refund on the price of our admission to the grounds, which surprised me so that I proceeded to buy six balls of orange-scented soap. Everything we did was satisfying, but the picnic was the highlight of our day.

pickling

The sign said "Pickling Cukes for Sale." I had stopped at the vegetable stand for squash, but seeing the sign I wondered if perhaps I didn't want some pickling cukes too. I hadn't made pickles for three or four years, not since before Grammy B. died. She and I used to make them together, sharing the labor and the satisfaction. We made Bread and Butter pickles, cutting small cucumbers into thin slices, cooking them with sliced onions and chopped peppers in a solution of vinegar, sugar and spices. I thought about the wonderful smell of hot vinegar and spices. It was evocative of autumn and farm house kitchens dominated by big, black stoves. Yes, I decided, I definitely should get some pickling cukes.

"Will there be anything else?" asked the farmer after weighing my squash.

"I see you have pickling cukes."

"That's right. I've got lots of them." He went into a back room and brought out a large wooden box filled to the brim with cucumbers. "Two dollars for the box," he said.

"That's a lot of cucumbers," I commented indecisively.

"Yes, and they're all fresh — just picked this morning." Looking them over I could see they were all sizes.

"I don't know. They're not as small as I'd like." But even as I spoke I was thinking of other pickles I could make besides the Bread and Butter.

"Oh, there's lots of little ones in there," he urged. I took a deep breath.

"Okay, I'll take the box." He dumped the cucumbers into a fifty pound potato bag, and it was full.

When I got home I spread the cucumbers out on the porch floor and divided them into piles by size. I was a bit overwhelmed to discover how many I had bought for my two dollars and the wide range in their sizes. This was not the carefully picked bushel of small, evenly sized cucumbers that Grammy B. used to order from a local farmer. There were quite a few small ones, but there were fat ones and some were very large and tinged with yellow. Obviously this was an end-of-the season crop.

I brought my cookbook and recipe box out onto the porch. Sitting on the floor I went through pickle recipes deciding what kinds I would make and making a list of other ingredients I would need. I decided to use some of the smallest cukes for a batch of Nicky's Pickles. These are small, whole cucumbers packed in a brine of vinegar, brown sugar, dry mustard, and spices. One of the nice things about Nicky's Pickles is that they don't have to be cooked. And I decided I would make mustard pickles and Sengfurken, a ripe cucumber pickle, as well as the Bread and Butter.

After lunch, which was a cucumber sandwich, I checked the barrel in the shed where I keep my canning jars and found that I had more quart size than pints, but that didn't present a problem as the Sengfurken would be long, thin strips that would pack nicely in quart jars. I recalled, happily, Grammy B's discovery during our last pickle-making session that the dishwasher does a beautiful job of sterilizing the jars. The process of boiling bottles on the stove could be eliminated.

I went to the supermarket and bought white and brown sugar, vinegar, dry mustard, turmeric, celery seed, onions, green peppers, coarse salt, jar rubbers, and cauliflower, and some small, white onions — these last for the mustard pickles.

"Wow," said Jamie when he came home from school. "Look at all the cucumbers." He had a cucumber sandwich for his snack and then helped me put the cucumbers in paper bags.

I made up Nicky's Pickles before supper. I washed about forty small cukes and packed them into clean gallon jars. The girls and their friend Sue came in while I was mixing the brine. They watched me pour it over the cukes.

"We'll have to shake these jars every day," I said.

"Is that all there is to it? Pickles are easy to make," said Stephanie. I offered no comment thinking of the other recipes I had to follow.

After supper I started the Bread and Butter pickles. I had, I estimated, about two pecks of cucumbers that were the right size. The recipe called for eight cups of sliced cucumbers. One peck equals eight quarts. I wondered if one quart of sliced cukes was the same as one quart of whole cukes. I checked the table of weights and measures in the back of my cookbook and discovered that four quarts equal eight pounds. Perhaps I could weigh the whole cukes and determine how many cups of sliced cukes I'd have. I brought the baby scales down from the attic and weighed the cukes. After much figuring and some measuring of sliced cucumbers I decided that two pecks of cucumbers equaled about eight times the recipe. That meant I had to slice up sixty-four cups of cucumbers and sixteen cups of onions.

The sliced vegetables had to be covered with salt and left to sit overnight. The salt would draw the water out of them. I wondered what I had for a pan that was large enough to hold all those vegetables and all that water. The answer turned out to be the cut glass punch bowl.

A good Bread and Butter pickle is made with thinly sliced cucumbers. Fat, uneven slices will not do. My fingers grew tired holding the small, firm cucumbers, but my hands worked with a rhythm. Lop, lop went the stem ends; zip, zip went the knife sectioning the cucumber on the cutting board; swish went the quarter-sized rounds into the punch bowl. After cutting up half of the cukes I switched to the onions and had a good cry for myself. When I had filled a cup sixteen times with sliced onions I was ready to go back to the cucumbers. The sliced vegetables filled the punch bowl to the brim. I sprinkled them with coarse salt and went to bed.

In the morning the kitchen smelled of onions and the clear, fresh smell of raw vegetables. The cucumbers and onions had settled in the bowl and were covered with water. I poured the water off and rinsed the vegetables three or four times. I chopped the green peppers, using one or two red ones for color, and added them to the cucumbers and onion. The vegetables looked like Christmas in the punch bowl.

In a large enamel kettle I mixed vinegar, sugar, celery seed, and turmeric. I added the vegetables, stirred them with a wooden spoon and left them to cook for twenty minutes. While the cucumbers turned a pale, jewel-like shade of green, the jars that were to receive them were being washed and sterilized in the dishwasher. I sat at the kitchen table having a cup of coffee and enjoying the aroma that rose out of the kettle. This too was part of the ritual. All I missed was Grammy B. and our chatter about how worthwhile a project this was despite the cost and the work.

When it was time to jar the pickles I was a little nervous and it took me two or three jars to get into the swing of the process. Out of the dishwasher came a steaming jar, out of a pan of boiling water came a jar rubber. My fingers jumped away from the hot glass and rubber as I fitted the red ring over the neck of the jar, being careful to put the lip, which would be used to break the seal when it was pickle-eating-time, away from the wire clamp. Into the jar went a wide-mouthed funnel and then I scooped the hot pickles into the jar, filling it to the brim. I was careful to wipe all the tiny celery seeds off the rim before fitting a glass cover into place. I clamped the wires and turned the jar upside down to set the seal. When I was done I had sticky pickle juice all over my hands, the counter, the stove, every utensil in sight, and the twenty-four pints of pickles which stood on their heads on the table.

By the time the children came home from school the pickles were cool. They watched me unclamp each jar to test its seal. They were glad when I found one seal broken, for this meant they could taste the pickles. Stephanie helped me wipe the sticky jars clean while Leslie wrote out a label for each one. Jamie helped me carry the gleaming jars into the cellar to be lined up on the shelves that had stood empty for so long.

On the next day and the next I made the mustard pickles and the Sengfurken. I became heartily sick of cucumbers before I was done, but when the last jar of pickles had been put in the cellar I felt the satisfaction a squirrel must feel when he has stored away his acorns for the winter. We will not subsist on the pickles, but they will brighten our winter in many ways. Grammy Dot will have a jar or two for her bridge club luncheons. On Thanksgiving morning the children will go into the cellar to choose the pickles that we will eat with our turkey. And Aunt Dotty will get pickles under the Christmas tree. The value of homemade pickles does not lie just in the eating of them.

tuesday

Tuesday was a glorious day. The air was cool but the day was warm with the splash and glow of fall foliage. Maple trees blazed red and orange, oaks burned bronze and yellow. Crisp, spiney firs and pines gave contrast and texture where they stood beside the deciduous trees. The sky was a brilliant blue; not a wash, but a strong blue, a mat for the white clouds that seemed inflated by the wind that swept the tree tops, pulling at leaves that were not ready to give up their season on the bough. Tuesday was a day for crying:

> O world, I cannot hold thee close enough!
>
> . . . .
>
> Thy woods, this autumn day, that ache and sag
> And all but cry with color!
>
> . . . .
>
> World, World, I cannot get thee close enough!*

But I did not have the time or inclination for such a call on Tuesday, for that was the day I went to Park Street School to see a film about people who molest children.

A notice about the film came home from school. It had been shown to the PTA and the feeling there had been that the children should see it. We have reason in our town to know that the child molester is a real and present danger. The notice, telling that the film would be shown, asked that parents come to school to see it with their children. And so we gathered, arriving just after lunch, parking our cars along the street by the school, passing up the walk under the bright flag strung taut on its pole by the wind, greeting our friends, coming together as we had done in the past to watch our children perform puppet shows or to hear them sing.

Inside the school I went to Stephanie's room to get her, and we went down to the auditorium together. The lunch tables were still set up although the serving windows to the kitchen were closed. We took a seat at one of the tables and watched the janitor setting up rows of chairs for the many parents coming in with their children.

Always before when parents had been invited to school during the day just the mothers had come. But this time there were fathers too. In some cases both parents accompanied a child. I wondered if having the fathers present said to the children as it did to me, "This is different. This isn't just another program. Something serious is happening here."

While Stephanie and I waited for the film to begin she pointed out to me two large Halloween murals at the front of the room that had been made by a sixth grade class. They were pictures of gloomy houses, lumpy graveyards, sailing moons, slinky cats and witches, owls, bats, ghosties and ghoulies — all the scary things that children delight in because they are not real.

"And then there are the real dangers," I thought.

The auditorium filled up rapidly. Ahead of us a mother lifted a

*From *Collected Poems* Harper and Row. Copyright 1917, 1945 by Edna St. Vincent Millay.

loose strand of hair out of her daughter's face, tucking it into her barrette. All around us children shuffled their feet, swung their legs against the benches they sat on, scratched and wiggled. These unconscious gestures, in contrast to the solid, self-containment of their parents, underlined the vulnerability of children.

Before the film was shown the president of the PTA talked briefly. The movie's purpose was, he said, to educate not to frighten. The people in it were professional actors. Although the business of educating children against the dangers of the child molester was up to the parents it was felt that this film might help the children understand. He reminded the children that they must never get into a stranger's car. They must not take presents of any kind from strangers. They should stay away from empty buildings and public toilets.

"Never let strangers pat you or hold you or unbutton your clothes," he said. In front of me two little girls who were sitting together giggled, surprised and a little embarrassed that anyone would say such a thing in front of so many people.

The movie began with a scene on a playground. A little girl was playing hopscotch. The shadow of a man fell across the squares she had chalked on the ground. The man held out a bag of candy, and the little girl smiled up at him. Behind me a small voice said, "Is that a stranger?"

"That is a stranger," warned a woman's quiet voice. "And you don't· go with strangers."

My mind wandered from the film even though I saw it all. I was not with the little girl in the picture, but with the girl who was found in Kennebunk this summer. What I was seeing was too close to what we all had had on our minds since we'd first heard that she was missing. We had hedged our thoughts and feelings, afraid to think of the child's ordeal, not wanting to speculate on just what had been done to her (for somehow this was an infringement on her family's privacy and grief), wanting her family to know that we agonized for them, and asking ourselves, "How could I bear it if that golden haired child on the verge of womanhood had been mine?" Because of the loss of that child — snatched from our pre-occupied midst — we all dealt privately with the fearful question of how to face with our own children the evil fact that people with sick minds live among us.

What place do these people have in our world of love, felicity, and beauty? The answer is that they make their place with cunning and singlemindedness and those of us with normal appetites and needs do not perceive them, for such warped minds can go undetected easily. Therefore those of us whose young are potential prey must give them defenses against the molester. We must intrude upon our children's innocence with cruel facts. We must sully their childish notions of ghosts and goblins with specific information about real demons. Understanding this we take time on a glorious fall day — the kind of day that speaks to poets and painters — to see with our children a film about a little girl who is taken from a playground to a lonely wood where she is chased relentlessly until she is caught.

the elms

The elms are really lost to us. I can see that now, and I can accept it. There was a time when I did not want to admit that fact and felt that the elms could be saved. But I accept their loss now, and with grace, and this is so because of the new trees.

New trees are everywhere. They have been planted under the great skeletal remains of the elms. They look so spindly, so inconsequential. But I see more strength in them than I do even in the elm trees that are still healthy. Even the elms that are still green look ragged and tired to me. What was it Dylan Thomas wrote . . .

> The force that through the green fuse drives the flower
> Drives my green age. . .*

That green fuse is in the innocent saplings. Their modest clusters of leaves belie tenacious roots that have established themselves in the ground and in time will encroach upon the hoary, rotting roots of the elms.

Now that the elms are dead and dying I want them gone. I wish I could pluck them out as I do flowers in the garden that have passed their prime. Since they had to die all at once I wish we could be done with them quickly instead of having to go through the slow process of seeing them marked with red crosses, of the laborious noisy cutting that litters the ground with twigs broken like shattered icicles. It is too bad that we will have to see the elms in the fields disintegrate gradually, losing their bark and dropping craggy limbs as wind and ice storms decree.

When the jagged remains of the elms no longer finger the sky we will see what our town looked like in the beginning when the mansions were just being built and their bulk rose against blue sky. I have caught glimpses of this vista already, and it is a clean, fresh view. It gives me a feeling of beginning again, as the young can, with unsullied ideals and untested plans.

Thomas' poem says that the same force that drives youth will also be youth's destroyer.

> The force that through the green fuse drives the
>   flower
> Drives my green age; that blasts the roots of trees
> Is my destroyer.
> And I am dumb to tell the crooked rose
> My youth is bent by the same wintry fever.

This is nature's way. Youth evolves into age; the old must make way for the young — sooner or later. The elms had to go. The beetles have hurried their passing, and we have had to suffer their loss all at once instead of gradually, but the elms would have gone eventually anyway. It is nature's way.

This means, of course, that someday the new trees will die too: the showy maples, the elegant birch, the slender ash, the decorative willow. But hopefully I won't have to see that. It has been hard enough to see the elm trees die. As much as I am appeased by the new young trees, their promise does not erase the regret I feel for the elms. The saplings will in time fill up the sky as the elm trees did, but with different forms and style. So it is when generations supersede generations. I think I'm glad that as the age of a tree compares with the age of a human being, chances are very good that I will not see the next generation of saplings planted in this town.

gramps' trip

We went to John's for Thanksgiving, and we took Gramps with us. John is living in Pennsylvania now so the trip was a special one for Gramps who has lived all of his life in Maine, leaving it only once or twice to go south as far as Boston, and having been beyond that point only once, years ago, to visit his Uncle Harry in Hartford, Connecticut.

We planned to leave here at dawn on a Wednesday morning so Gramps drove down from his home the day before. He arrived late in the afternoon, looking very special in a black three-quarter length coat, black hat set with a Tyrolean cockade, a handsome yellow tattersall shirt, nubbly sport coat and new slacks. He had come by turnpike from Augusta, and when I asked him if he'd had a good trip the answer was, "Yes, but boy don't they drive! I was going 55 or 60 and they went by me as if I was tied. They drive too fast."

Supper that night was lobster, a treat for Gramps who said it was the first lobster he'd had this year. Throughout the meal and into the evening it was pleasant to listen to him tell about his annual hunting trip.

"Didn't get my deer," he said. "Only saw one, a small doe. I went into Richmond Pond, way in, and that's where I saw her. She jumped up right in front of me and was gone into the brush before I could get her in my sights. I went up the side of Bald Mountain further than I'd ever gone, and I found a beautiful stand of beech. Don't believe there'd ever been a blade in that grove. Beautiful trees. I take my little tin cup with me when I hunt and if I get thirsty I just find a stream and scoop up a cupful of water. The water is sparkling clear, but I don't know how long it will be that way. There're more and more people coming into the state all the time. They want to get away from the cities, but I don't know how long it will be different up here. Remember my trip to Boston four years ago? I wouldn't care if I never went again. Race and rush, day and night. Why, they live around the clock down there!

When I came home and turned onto Pond Road I was so happy. It was peaceful and quiet." Listening to Gramps, I wondered if he would enjoy the trip into Megalopolis.

Wednesday morning the alarm went off at 5 a.m. We got up and went about our preparations with that feeling of reluctance and anticipation that comes with an early morning rising for a special reason. We had oatmeal for breakfast, and as we sat at the table Jamie launched into a singing of "Good morning to you, good morning to you; we're all in our places with sun-shiny faces. . ."

"For heaven's sake," said Gramps. "Are they still singing that song in school?"

By the time we were ready to go, the light of day had begun to rise. We stepped into a beautiful world. Hoarfrost covered everything; even the air seemed grey with it. When we turned onto the River Road we looked across the pasture to see the sky banded with pink and rose like pulled taffy, and looking the other way we saw the white moon waiting in the grey sky. The lights were on in Mr. Moulton's barn and they seemed to offer assurance that our world would carry on even though we were leaving it. The ticket we picked up at the entrance to the turnpike was stamped 6:28 a.m. We turned South and were on our way.

Our sense of excitement, anticipation, and accomplishment grew the further south we went. By the time we reached Connecticut the traffic was heavy.

"You wonder where all the people are going, don't you," said Gramps. We passed tobacco fields and drying sheds weathered to a rich brown. "For heaven's sake, I never knew they grew tobacco in Connecticut," said Gramps. When we saw the buildings of downtown Hartford on the horizon he said, "I haven't been to Hartford since I was a kid and went down to visit Uncle Harry."

From that point on Gramps' wonder at our progress gave us all pleasure. When we came to signs for Greenwich, Connecticut, he asked, "Is this the place you read about where all the hippies live?"

"No," Bob told him. "That's Greenwich Village in New York City."

"You really ought to see New York, Dad," I said.

"I'd probably walk around with my mouth open and be disgusted," he answered, and then added, "They say anything happens in New York City you just mind your own business and keep right on going."

We crossed the state line into New York. "Are we in New York?" asked Gramps.

"That's right."

"For heaven's sake!" When we crossed the line into New Jersey he said, "Now I'm in New Jersey." At that point Gramps' wonderment reached Jamie who asked, "Are we halfway around the world?" We crossed the Delaware River into Pennsylvania.

"Now I'm in Pennsylvania," said Gramps.

Our vacation in Pennsylvania was satisfying. We had the pleasure of being together in John's home for Thanksgiving. We liked the old-world flavor of the countryside with its narrow roads, the expansive cornfields harvested to a brown stubble, mockingbirds in the air, pheasant in the hedgerows, stone houses on the horizon flanked by Osage orange trees. We visited Amish country and in one of their market places we bought home-cured bacon, and Jamie selected an early Christmas present for me: a small pot of Baby's Tears ground cover. On another day we visited a place called Peddlar's Village, a shopping center of specialty shops, and saw the spectacle of affluent America shopping. We saw a lot in two days time.

On Saturday morning we headed home — by way of New York City. We had decided that Gramps should see The City. Chances were that he would never come this way again. We followed the Jersey Pike out of Trenton. The smog was heavy. The air was green and yellow with it. A plane just overhead was soon lost to sight and steel towers supporting high tension wires on either side of the highway were barely visible at a distance of 500 yards. We saw most clearly, it seemed, the stacks of factories belching smoke into the already thick air. We saw rows of apartment houses in shrouded lines beside the highway and Gramps said, "Life doesn't mean anything here does it."

We could not see the skyline of New York, a disappointment, but one of the children peering intently at the smog said suddenly, "Look, there's the Statue of Liberty."

"Where?" asked Gramps, sitting on the edge of his seat. We looked and saw her outline, a towering figure even in the distance.

"So that's the Statue of Liberty," said Gramps. "I never thought I'd see that. Yes sir, that's the Statue of Liberty. I'm glad you spied that." He watched her out of sight.

We crossed under the Hudson River through the Holland Tunnel. We drove into The City. The air was, surprisingly, clear, and oh such sights we saw: the Empire State Building seemingly on every side as we turned and maneuvered in the streets, the spectacle of Christmas lights and Christmas shoppers, horse drawn hacks on the fringes of Central Park, and vendors on every corner selling pretzels and roasted chestnuts.

We parked the car in a garage near the Taft Hotel and walked around the Time-Life building, Radio City Music Hall, and into Rockefeller Center to see the skaters under the golden Prometheus. Gramps stopped again and again to look up at the skyscrapers. After lunch we picked up the car, and our way home led us through Harlem with its rows of concrete door stoops and its asphalt playgrounds. It seemed we rode forever before we finally left The City behind us.

"This has been the trip of my lifetime," said Gramps.

Our counting of state lines began again: Connecticut at last, after a long ride, Massachusetts. Night came, and we pushed on. When we crossed into New Hampshire, our watching began in earnest. And then we were over the Portsmouth bridge and into Kittery, Maine, and before us, shining out of the night, was the sign MAINE TURNPIKE. We passed under its light and broke into a cheer and then sang:

> Grand State of Maine, proudly we sing,
> To tell your glories to the world
> And shout your praises till the echoes ring.
> Should fate unkind, send us to roam,
> The scent of the fragrant pine, the tang of the salty sea,
> Will call us home.
> Oh Pine Tree State, your woods, fields and hills
> Your lakes, streams and rock-bound coast
> Will ever fill our hearts with thrills.
> And though we seek far and wide
> Our search will be in vain
> To find a fairer spot on earth
> Than MAINE, MAINE, MAINE*

And Gramps from the back seat sang softly, "Raise the steins to dear old Maine..." We were glad to be home.

*State of Maine Song

the hiding place

The children are trying to find my Hiding Place; the place where I keep the presents. I can hear them upstairs tap, tap, tapping along the walls. They are looking for a secret panel. They giggle as they go from room to room, for their search is more game than not, even though they are indeed reduced to suspecting that the Hiding Place is behind a secret panel. They have known for a long time that there is a special place for presents and they have speculated about it and even looked for it. But they have not found it. The Hiding Place is still my secret, for which I am thankful, especially at Christmastime.

I secrete presents in the Hiding Place throughout the year — birthday presents, special surprises — but it is at Christmastime that I use it most, squirreling away treasures and trinkets for Christmas morning. Many of the children's treasures came to them by way of the Hiding Place. Jamie's Winnie-the-Pooh waited there as did the eight-inch antique doll in the blue dress who sits now on the top shelf in Stephanie's room. I have hidden furry muffs there and music boxes. And books: *The Yearling* for Leslie, poetry for Steph, and Jamie's copy of *The Cricket in Times Square*. The bamboo cricket cage and the wooden cricket that were my personal gift to Jamie last Christmas were hidden in the Hiding Place. Scarves, stationery, mittens, and sweaters that come out of the Hiding Place are perfumed, for The Place has held, over the years, scented soap, boxes of powder, and vials of perfume. If the children ever discover my secret cache they'll know it, for it bears the scent of Christmas past.

Because the children understand that I need The Place their efforts to find it are half-hearted, but they do like to talk about it. Tonight Leslie asked me, "Have you got any presents in your hiding place yet?"

"Oh, yes," I answered. "Quite a few."

"I wonder where it is," breathed Stephanie.

"I'll bet I know," said Jamie. "If I guess will you tell me, Mama?" I shrugged. "Maybe. ."

"Is it ..."

"Wait! Whisper in my ear." There was always the chance that he could guess. He came and whispered, "On the shelf in your bedroom closet."

"Oh no," I said aloud. "I only put wrapped presents on the closet shelf."

"And under your bed," said Leslie. "I found some presents there last year."

"Wrapped presents. I put the unwrapped presents in the Hiding Place."

"It's not the cedar chest in the attic," said Stephanie.

"That never was the Hiding Place," I said. "I did used to put some things there, but not anymore; not since you found the doll."

"Yes, but I was only little," Steph explained.

"I know!" cried Jamie, who had been thinking. "The shelf in the cellar way."

"Of course not," scoffed Leslie. "That's where the cats sleep." Jamie's outcry had shaken me.

"Stop talking about it," I said. "It's making me nervous."

"Someday will you tell me?" asked Leslie.

"When you're grown up and gone away."

"Not till then?"

"When you live in East Oshkosh I'll write you a letter and say, 'Dear Leslie, The Hiding Place is ...' ."

"Dear Leslie," said Stephanie in her Flip Wilson voice. "The Hiding Place is ... the chimney."

"Don't tease, Stephanie," said Leslie. "I really want to know."

"No you don't," I said. "Just think how hard it would be wanting to look and trying not to. Anyway, even if you knew it wouldn't do you any good. I've got it rigged with an electric eye like they've got at the drugstore." Jamie's eyes opened wide.

"Oh, Mama," said Leslie. "You're just kidding."

"No I'm not. If anyone finds it bells will ring and sirens will sound."

"Errrrrrrr," said Jamie, who's sound effects are realistic.

"It must be a trap door," said Stephanie. "Or a secret panel. That's what it is! There's a secret panel in this house that only you and Daddy know about."

"Come on," said Jamie. "Let's go find it." They flew upstairs to tap along the walls.

The tapping has stopped now, but I'm sure the speculation has not. The children are doing their homework, and I suspect that thoughts of Christmas treasures intrude upon their geography and math. Tis the season!

the pageant

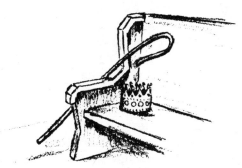

The pageant has been accomplished; now we can have Christmas. Mary can braid up her hair and help frost cookies. Freckle-faced Joseph can think about going for the Christmas tree. The youngest angels can make plans for the dolls they hope to find under the tree. The littlest shepherd can give himself over to enjoying the glitter and sweet abundance of the season, and all the other angels, shepherds, and the townspeople can be just themselves: noisy, bright-eyed children getting ready for the holiday. They can have their feasting and presents now and so can I, and my Christmas will be richer than it would have been without the pageant.

The children came together a few days before Christmas Sunday to rehearse the pageant which was to be presented at the 11 o'clock Sunday morning service. They came into the quiet of the sanctuary trailing snow, bright stocking caps, and laughter. The little girls were prim or shy, the youngest boys pushed and shoved one another in jest, the older girls and boys who had the speaking parts appeared more thoughtful about their purpose in being there. As director of the pageant I rushed about, a sheaf of papers in my hand, hoping to bring order out of confusion.

"Let's be quiet now so we can get started," I called. "Where is Mary? Joseph, are you here? Innkeeper, is your daughter with you? Have all the kings arrived? Okay, let's be quiet so we can assign the other parts. Who would like to be an angel?" A bevy of little girls immediately gathered around me, and one small boy who said in a loud voice, "I want to be an angel."

"We'd like that very much," I told him. Two fourth grade girls wondered if they were too old to be angels. While they made the difficult decision, I rounded up the shepherds. Most of the younger boys wanted to be shepherds. The children who were left, of all ages and sizes, were townspeople.

"Everyone come and get a costume," I called. "Mrs. Adams will help you." The costumes looked meagre. They were simple tunics made from strips of corduroy and denim. The angels' costumes were made from white sheets. Mary's draperies were pale blue sheeting. The kings' regalia — someone's discarded drapes, a choir robe, handsome strips of brocade, and crowns made from pieces of velvet and gold paper decorated with sequins, seemed surprisingly elegant.

"All right," I said. "I want all the angels here in this pew. Shepherds stop running and come sit here. Townspeople here. Is everyone ready now? Then listen. We'll start at the back. While the congregation sings "O Come, O Come Emmanuel" you will take your places for the pageant. Mary and Joseph you sit in the front pew on the right. Shepherds stay in the back at the right. Angels, you go up into the choir loft, all except Gabriel . . . you stay down front across the aisle from Mary. Innkeeper, you and your daughter sit on the stairs to the choir loft out of sight. Townspeople, you go to the front on the right and on the left. Kings, you sit still for now. We're going to run through this roughly once. Innkeeper, I can see your head. Townspeople, stop talking and listen. I'll be the Narrator. I'll be at the back, and I will begin by saying . . .:"

Many years ago a very strange and wonderful thing happened. And the strange part is that it has never been forgotten, and the wonderful thing is that it told of perfect love, and peace, and hope for a better world.

"Now Mary, you get up and go forward and sit on the stool. Gabriel, you go and stand by her.

Narrator: It all began when an angel appeared to a young woman.
Angel Gabriel: Mary, do not be afraid for you have found favor with God.
Mary: What do you mean?
Angel G.: You are going to have a son and you will call Him Jesus.
Mary: How can that be? I have no husband.
Angel G.: Your child will be a Holy Child, and He will be called the Son of God.
Mary: I still do not understand, but I believe in the love of God, and if this is what He asks of me I am content.

"You must speak up, Mary," I said. "We want to hear you from the back. Gabriel, you go now and join the other angels. Mary, you

must sit on your stool while we all look at you and the soloist sings
'Lo How a Rose Ere Blooming'." Mary blushed, and the shepherds
tittered.

After the solo the Narrator told how the angel appeared to
Joseph and how after their marriage, when Mary was great with
child, the Emperor Augustus sent out a decree that all the people
must register for the census. So Joseph and Mary joined the
crowds of people traveling to the town of Bethlehem. While the
organist played "O Little Town of Bethlehem" the townspeople
and Mary and Joseph walked up the side aisle, across the back of
the church and down the center aisle. "Remember, you are tired,"
I prompted.

The townspeople ended up where they started from, and Mary
and Joseph approached the steps to the choir loft where they were
met by the Innkeeper and his daughter.

> Innkeeper: What do you want?
> Joseph: Do you have a room for my wife and me?
> We are very tired.
> Innkeeper: I'm sorry, but we're full.
> Joseph: Don't you have any place at all? My wife is ill
> . . .
> Innkeeper: Sorry, there's nothing we can do. (Joseph
> and Mary turn dejectedly to leave.)
> I. Daughter: Excuse me sir. We have a stable out back if
> that would be all right. The warmth of the animals will
> make it comfortable.
> Joseph: Thank you. You are very kind.
> Narrator: And so they went to the stable in Bethlehem.
> And there Mary gave birth to a son and they named
> Him Jesus.

"Now everyone will sing 'Away In A Manger'," I explained.
"Gabriel, while we're singing you bring one or two of the smallest
angels and come down to kneel by the creche."

"Are we supposed to sing too?" asked Joseph.

"No, the spotlight will be on you people. You must just pose for
us." And so it went. A quartet of recorders were played as the
shepherds came forward to the hills of Judea at the front of the
church. The shepherds cowered when a bright light appeared in
the choir loft and the First Angel appeared to them.

> First Angel: Do not be afraid. I bring you news of great
> joy . . .

"First Angel," I interrupted her. "We want to see your pretty face. Come forward and turn to the congregation a little. Yes, that's better."

> Narrator: And suddenly there were many angels in the
> heaven. They were praising God and saying, "Peace on
> earth ... good will to men."

The little angels came out of the choir loft and stood at the altar rail. "Peace on earth," they quavered, and then, mixing their men and good will, they stopped in confusion. All except for the little boy who staunchly carried through, "good will to men."

The news that the angels brought spread, and while the choir sang "Go Tell It On The Mountain" from the back of the church, the townspeople and shepherds moved again around the church and came to kneel near Mary and Joseph. And then the wise men came, one at a time, bearing, rather self-consciously, their gifts. They stood with bowed heads by the gathering at the front of the church and the tableau was complete.

"That's not bad," I told them. "Let's go through it now with no interruption and see how we do." The second run was as rough in some ways as the first. One group of townspeople forgot what to do. Mary's voice was softer, and she drooped a little with fatigue. The shepherds whispered, and the kings slouched with boredom as they waited for their turn. The First Angel forgot to project to the audience, and the choir missed a cue. But I dismissed the children.

"Be here at 10:30 Sunday morning. Angels, you'll get your halos and wings then. Have your costumes ironed. And don't worry about this. You're going to be great."

And they were. The angels spoke their line perfectly even though the one little boy angel, realizing he was the only boy in that bevy, became instead a townsperson. Mary was serene. First Angel didn't forget to turn to the congregation. The kings were regal. The costumes were amazingly effective: the little boys robed in denim and scraps of bright cloth did indeed look like Biblical shepherds abiding in the fields. The flurry of townspeople passing up the aisles reminded me of Brueghel's painting, "The Census." The effectiveness of the pageant is one of the recurring miracles of Christmastime.

Somehow I can never sing the carols during the pageant. Sentiment overwhelms me, and I just hum. It is the lovely simplicity of the lines and the composure of the children that touch me. I love sweet Mary and her young Joseph, idealized as they are. I love the little angels with crooked halos who lean their elbows on the altar rail. I love the shepherds whose staffs are taller than they. I love seeing the eighth-grade boys playing at being kings. I love them all. At the end I find I am able to sing "Silent Night" and to receive with charity the Narrator's last words:

> And so it was. And so it is today. A child was born, a Holy Child. And so they came, and we come today to bow down before the Prince of Peace who was and is the hope of all mankind, and the Saviour of our world.

a new year

It was three o'clock in the afternoon before I stopped to think that this was the last day of the year. What had I done with it, this last day of 1969 and of the decade? Had it been a special day, marked by pageantry, music and bells, by solemn ceremony and deliberate leave taking?

In the morning after Bob had left for work and the children had gone out to slide, I wrote out the menus for the coming week and then went grocery shopping. I was pleased to find coffee on special — two pounds for $1.49, but eggs were still high at 83 cents a dozen. I brought home the usual staples and a few special purchases, among these a meaty shin bone for a vegetable soup.

It was close to noon when I got home so I fixed lunch as I put the six bags of groceries away. The children thought lunch a long time in coming. After eating they found dry socks and mittens and went out again. I cleared away the lunch dishes, spread the morning's wet mittens on the kitchen radiator to dry, let a cat out and the dog in, put a load of wash in the machine, and started the soup.

I wished that I had a big, black stove in my kitchen so I could simmer the bone all afternoon with a bay leaf and some celery leaves, but lacking such a stove I put the bone into the pressure cooker. While it cooked I diced onions, carrots, celery, turnip, and chopped up a big piece of cabbage. Rummaging for the celery in the vegetable drawer I found a cache of apples that were too old for crisp eating, but too good to throw away. I decided they should be made into applesauce, so set them aside for quartering.

The washer had finished its cycle so I put the clean clothes into the dryer and put another load of dirty clothes in to wash. The children came in and wanted cocoa, so Leslie got out the milk and cocoa while Stephanie and Jamie found room on the radiator for the second batch of wet mittens and socks, creating in spots two layers of wet wool.

The buzzer rang telling me the soup bone should come out of the pot. I skimmed the fat from the broth and added the vegetables. It was already an aromatic mixture. I thought how good crusty bread and cold butter would taste with it and decided to make bread. As I put the milk on to scald I wondered if perhaps it wasn't too late in the day to start bread, and that is when I realized that it was three o'clock. If I went ahead with the bread I would be waiting for it to rise through the evening and smelling its warm aroma as the year turned. It would be, I decided, a comfortable sort of vigil to keep on New Year's Eve, so I turned the heat on under the milk.

I finished the soup, adding last of all tomatoes and spices and then put it into the refrigerator. We'll have it tomorrow when the flavor of the vegetables has permeated the broth. Our supper went into the oven a little later than it should have and the sky was pale, as a winter sky is just before dusk, when I finally got to the apples. The sauce needed sugar and lemon juice and cinnamon. It will be good for breakfast.

It was dark outside when at last I sat down at the kitchen table to rest a minute. I took Eve the Cat on my lap and rubbed her white chin and the down behind her ears until she stuck out the tip of her pink tongue and her purr rumbled and rolled in her furry throat. The smell of our baking supper began to seep out of the oven, mixing with the smell of wet wool from the mittens on the radiator.

The nativity figures on the wide window sill posed in tableau against the darkness beyond the pane, and above them the silver star we pasted on the end of a thin thread twirled in the heat of the room. The last day of the year, and decade, was almost over. It had been an ordinary day. But the years are made up mostly of ordinary days and therein lies our greatest wealth, even though it is difficult to gain such a perspective on soup bones and wet mittens.

In the darkened dining room the table was set for supper, and in the front room Leslie put her new Christmas record on the player. I listened to words of the song. They promised that a new age was dawning, an age of love, understanding, sympathy, and trust; an age to fill every ideal of peace. I wonder if tomorrow _will_ be the dawning of a new age of harmony and understanding? It will at least be the beginning of a new year.

chicago

Chicago doesn't exist. It is an ad man's dream foisted off onto the American public. Or so I thought for a while last week.

Bob had business in Chicago, and I went along for the trip. We flew out of Boston at noon on Sunday. It was pleasant being on the plane. The studied but friendly sophistication of the stewardesses and the casual at-home attitude of many of the passengers gave me a sense of having stepped into a special stratum of society. We had stepped into an environment that is commonplace to some people even though it is far removed from our everyday life.

I felt a kinship with the other passengers, but found myself maintaining an aloof watchfulness. We all, I felt, were taking note of one another although no one smiled or even met the eyes of anyone else.

Boston harbor dropped slowly from view as a stewardess welcomed us, in a silky voice, over the intercom system.

"Good afternoon ladies and gentlemen. Welcome aboard. We will arrive in Chicago in approximately one hour and forty minutes. We wish you a pleasant flight."

"Imagine," I said. "Only an hour and a half to Chicago."

We settled in. A stewardess brought us sherry and our dinner. Two men across the aisle from us had Bloody Marys and seemed to have a lot to say to the prettiest stewardess. After eating we settled back to read the _New York Times_. It seemed we might for once get to read it all, for the only distraction here was the occasional by-play between the men across the aisle and the pretty stewardess.

We were well into our flight when the pilot announced, "Ladies and gentlemen, this is Captain Turner, your pilot. We are passing over the Finger Lakes region in New York state. It is snowing lightly in Chicago at this time, but we don't anticipate any difficulty. We expect to land on schedule." I returned to my reading. The pilot's next announcement came about an hour later after I had finished reading the book reviews, the magazine section, and was immersed in a front page news item about the discovery in Jerusalem of the skeleton of a man who had been crucified.

"We are in the Chicago area," said the pilot. "We're about 25 miles from the city. Conditions have deteriorated at O'Hare field. We'll be delayed a half hour or so in landing." I looked out of the window, but saw only clouds.

We held our flight pattern well over an hour. The monotony of the cloud-bound view, the drone of the engines which muted the chatter of the men across the aisle with the pretty stewardess, and the diminishing appeal of the *Times* was broken only once when the pilot announced, "Blanda just kicked a field goal. That makes it Baltimore 17, Oakland 10." The announcement served to underline my sense of detachment from the rest of the world. We were set apart, marooned in space, travelers facing interaction with one another like characters in a novel. The next announcement, when it came, was abrupt.

"We are flying on to Detroit to refuel. Then we'll try O'Hare again."

"Ever been to Detroit, Joyce?" Bob asked. Behind us there was a flurry of comment among the other passengers.

In Detroit some passengers got off the plane to stretch their legs or to make phone calls. Those of us who stayed on board found barriers between us dropping. Our common experience gave us something to talk about.

"Guess the winds are pretty high at O'Hare," said one of the men across the aisle. "Shirley says this pilot is pretty cautious. She's flown with him before, and he won't take any chances." We learned from our neighbor, and from Shirley, the pretty stewardess, that our plane had taken the last available gate at the Detroit airport. All incoming flights to Chicago were being diverted. We learned that there was no food or beverages aboard our plane, and the crowds of people in the terminal were quickly exhausting food supplies there. We noted that passengers returning to our plane were carrying candy bars.

"Want something to eat?" asked Bob.

"No, I'll have a steak when we get to Chicago." It was 5:30. We'd be in Chicago by eight for sure, not too late for dinner.

We sat in Detroit for almost four hours. Shirley had just finished telling us that she and the rest of the crew would soon be "illegal," that is, they would have been on duty the maximum number of hours allowed under flight regulations, when the pilot announced, "Ladies and gentlemen, we are going to leave in ten minutes for Chicago. We'll try again."

In the air we settled back to what diversions we could find. Shirley wrapped herself in a blanket and sat in the aisle at the feet of our neighbors.

"Aren't you going to serve us a steak dinner?" I asked.

"Here, want a candy bar?" asked the man on the aisle. I declined. It was dark outside. I plugged in the ear phones by my seat and leaned my head back to listen to Bach's "Shepherd's Cantata."

"Ladies and gentlemen," said the pilot. "We are now in a holding pattern over Chicago. It will be about ten minutes before the runways are plowed and ready for landings. We are one of about thirty planes waiting to land, but we're in a good slot — about number 9, so we should be down in about three quarters of an hour." A young father came up the aisle with his small son and disappeared into a lavatory. Half an hour later the pilot said, "They assure us it will only be twelve more minutes before the runways are cleared." The man across the aisle began to tap his fingers restlessly on the arm of his seat. A stewardess went by with a glass of water for someone. The earphones had begun to hurt my ears so I took them off. I wondered if our neighbor still had a candy bar to give away.

The pilot said, "We've been holding at 10,000 feet and now we've dropped to 6,000 so we *are* making progress. Wish I could tell you more, but communications are bad. Everyone is so busy. . ."

"I was supposed to fly a run to Mexico tomorrow," sighed Shirley.

"Do you still want to give that candy away?" I asked our neighbor. The little boy came by with his mother.

"Ladies and gentlemen," said the pilot. "O'Hare is closed. The runways are not plowed. We are proceeding to Indianapolis." A group in back who had been worried about making connections at O'Hare for Indianapolis cheered.

"Their problem is solved anyway," said Shirley. Someone cracked a joke about Indianapolis in the summer time.

We landed in a driving rain. It was 11 p.m. Luckily the coffee shop was still open, and we were able to get bacon and eggs. We shared a table with our companions from across the aisle and another passenger from our flight, a fashionably dressed young man whose cheerfulness belied the fatigue I felt and the tense control exhibited by our other mealmates. We introduced ourselves around as introductions seemed at last called for, and learned that our aisle companions were salesmen on their way to the carpet show in Chicago. The introductions were a subtle admission that chances were very good that we would see considerably more of one another before we were free to go our separate ways in Chicago. No one seemed bothered by this except Jack Sullivan, one of the carpet salesmen, who was fretting about not getting to the opening of the market.

We speculated about our fate as we ate our midnight supper. "What happens next?"

"They might put us on a bus for Chicago."

"That would be a four hour drive, longer if the roads are bad."

"The weather's bad all over. Shirley said they closed down Detroit after we left and landings in Cincinnati are doubtful because of thunderstorms in the area."

"Guess Chicago's having a real blizzard."

"They got some snow but the main problem at O'Hare is the wind."

"It doesn't take much snow to foul up Chicago. They don't know what to do with it.

"We're lucky to be down."

"I hope they don't put us on a bus."

"We could rent a car."

"There must be trains out of Indianapolis."

"Sometimes small planes can get into Chicago when jets can't," said Jack Sullivan.

"Right now I'm only interested in getting some sleep. Do you suppose they might fix us up with a room here?" And that is just what they did. We spent the night in Indianapolis, courtesy of the airline.

At 7 the next morning we joined a line at the ticket window hoping to get on a flight to Chicago. We were given standby tickets for an 8 o'clock flight. We sat in the lounge and hoped there would be room for us on the plane. Nearby a toddler in pink corduroy overalls pressed her nose against the plate glass window that looked out onto the field. "Choo, choo," she said to her mother.

"No, plane."

"Plane," she repeated happily and moved off down the lounge. "Come back, Megan," called her mother. Megan came back. She leaned on her mother's knee, looked up at her, and said, "Two, three."

"Four, five, six," recited her mother wearily. She was pregnant and obviously under more of a strain than the child. I smiled at the little girl and said to her mother, "She's doing very well."

"Yes. We left Newark at noon yesterday. She practically hasn't eaten since then. They ran out of milk on our plane. She hasn't slept much either."

"Children are tough," I said.

By 7:55 it was clear that there was not room for us on the 8:00 flight. The next flight was scheduled for 10:30, and we were told that reservations for it would not be taken until 9:30.

"Let's go get some breakfast," said Bob. We found a booth in the crowded coffee shop and ordered a hearty breakfast. In the next booth Megan's mother was trying to get her to drink some milk.

"Mommy, mommy, mommy," fussed Megan.

"This is a nightmare," said her mother.

After breakfast while I was buying a supply of candy bars and a Chicago paper, Bob got boarding passes for the 10:30 flight.

"What does that mean," I asked.

"That means we definitely get seats on the plane."

In the lounge we saw Megan and her parents.

"Did you get passes?" They had. We also saw one of the carpet salesmen and learned from him that Jack Sullivan had chartered a private plane to fly him into Chicago. Our other supper companion, the cheerful young man, was there, and a mix of people who had started their trip to Chicago from Newark, Boston, and Toronto. A frumpy woman whom we had noticed before because of her broken English and the after-ski boots she wore over charcoal knee lengths, noticed the headlines on the Chicago paper, which were, "Chicago Gets Foot of Snow. O'Hare Snarled."

"This 'snarled'. . .," she said. "What does it mean?"

"All mixed up," explained the pleasant young man. She nodded vigorously. She could understand that.

While we waited, Bob chatted with a hospital corpsman who was trying to return to his base at the Great Lakes Naval Training Center. I talked with a student whose home was in Chicago and who was worried about an exam he had scheduled for that afternoon. At 10:30 it was announced that the flight had been postponed until eleven because the plane had not yet been fueled. People all around us laughed or groaned.

"Why don't we go up?" asked the lady in the charcoal knee lengths.

"The excuse this time is that the fuel isn't in the plane yet," Bob told her. "They have a long list of excuses and they start at the top and work their way down." A pretty girl said, "When they run out of excuses maybe they'll let us on."

"Oh no," said Bob. "Then they'll go back to the top of the list."

The lady in knee lengths, who had been listening closely to this exchange, sucked in her breath.

"Don't listen to him," I said. "He's making a joke." To make jokes about our plight had become the thing to do.

The pleasant young man, who had been gazing absently out of the window onto the field said slowly, "Don't tell me they still use a wind sock at this airport. That must be our problem." And then as his thoughts crystalized he added brightly, "That's it. The wind sock is broken!" Everyone laughed except the lady in knee socks who looked puzzled.

Bob resumed his conversation with the corpsman, and I went to the ladies' room. Half a dozen women were there smoking and talking.

"I left Newark at noon yesterday," one was saying. "When I get to Chicago my friends will never believe me."

"Didn't you know?" I interrupted. "Chicago doesn't exist!" They looked at me in startled surprise, and then we all laughed together.

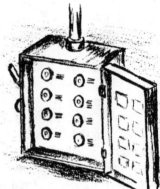

the noise

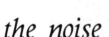

"Mama, there's a noise in my room," said Jamie.

"What kind of a noise?"

"I don't know." I went upstairs and listened. I didn't know what kind of a noise it was either. It was a persistent, pebbly noise that sort of hummed and almost vibrated. It seemed to be coming from inside the wall against which the bureau stood. There are two bracket lights on the wall that are almost old enough to be called antiques. I wondered if the noise came from their wiring; it had an electrical sound.

"We'll tell Dad about it when he gets home," I told Jamie.

When Bob got home I said, "There's a noise in Jamie's room."

"What kind of a noise?"

"I'm not sure. Go see what you think." When Bob came downstairs he said, "Sounds like it might be in the wiring of those old lights. After supper we'll shut off the juice in that room and see if it stops. This will give me a good chance to label the new fuse box." The fuse box had been put in during some recent remodeling.

After supper Bob said to the children, "I have to find out if the noise in Jamie's room is in the wiring and while I'm at it I want to label the new fuse box. Everyone is going to have to help. As I disconnect fuses you tell me what lights go out. Leslie, you stand at the top of the cellar stairs. Stephanie, you take the front rooms. Jamie, you cover the bathroom and all the bedrooms except your own. Joyce, you take Jamie's room and tell me if the noise stops when the lights go out."

We took our positions. From my place in the upstairs hall which runs between Jamie's room and the stairway down to the kitchen I heard Bob call from the cellar, "Ready?"

"Ready," Leslie answered from her position in the kitchen. Jamie and I waited at the top of the stairs.

"Nothing's happening," he said.

"It will," I assured him, and then we heard Stephanie call, "Living room lights out, front hall lights out." Leslie relayed the word down the cellar stairs.

"Living room lights out, front hall lights out."

"And the TV's stopped," called Steph. This was surprising for the television is in the family room. And, I wondered, why was the television set turned on anyway?

"The TV's off," Leslie called to her father.

"What?" I heard Bob ask from the depths of the house.

"Leslie," I said down the back stairs. "Daddy doesn't need to know that." Leslie passed my comment on to Stephanie who's reply was, "Living room lights on, front hall lights on."

"The living room lights are on again," Leslie told her father. Upstairs I tapped my foot restlessly and wondered how long it would take us to get through the whole house.

"Why don't the lights go out?" asked Jamie, who was restless too. At the foot of the stairs the kitchen went dark.

"The lights are out in the kitchen, the back hall, the laundry and Mama's room," Leslie called.

Jamie and I listened to the action downstairs as room after room was darkened and then illuminated. And then suddenly the bathroom and one bedroom went dark. Jamie sprang to action.

"Bathroom lights out, your bedroom lights out," he hollered at me. I sent the information down to Leslie.

When at last the lights went out in the upstairs hallway and Jamie's room I stood in the dark and listened to the noise. It sounded louder in the dark.

"The lights are out in Jamie's room but the noise hasn't stopped," I called to Leslie. Obviously our problem wasn't electrical, but what *was* causing the weird noise?

Later when we gathered in the kitchen again Stephanie said matter-of-factly, "It's mice."

I doubt it, Steph. At least, I haven't seen any signs of any in the house this year."

"Maybe it's a ghost," Leslie speculated playfully.

"Oh no," I told her. "If we had a ghost he'd have made himself known long before this." And then, seeing the thoughtful look on Jamie's face, I added firmly, "Of course it isn't a ghost."

It was Jamie's bedtime. When I came downstairs after saying goodnight I commented, "That's the oddest noise. In a way it sounds familiar. Do you suppose it *is* mice?"

"It could be, I suppose," said Bob.

"Daddy," called Jamie. "The noise changes."

"It will probably take him forever to get to sleep." But it seemed that even forever might not be long enough.

"Daddy," Jamie called again. "I can't sleep. The noise is bothering me." Bob went upstairs and put him and Winnie-the-Pooh to bed in our room.

At the end of the evening when Bob and I went upstairs we put the sleeping Jamie back into his own bed. The noise was still there, but we hoped it wouldn't wake him up. We stood in the dark room listening.

"That almost sounds like a chipmunk," I said. "You know how they chee-chee-chee from the tops of the trees. Maybe one got into the attic and somehow got down between the walls."

"If it's an animal it seems as though he'd stop and rest once in a while." Just then the noise shifted, going higher, blurring a little in transition and that's when I realized what it was.

"I know what it is," I said, going to the bureau. I opened the drawers one at a time and felt through their contents. In the bottom drawer under a pair of boxing gloves I found what I was looking for and brought it out, bumbling, in my hand.

"Jim's old walkie-talkie!" said Bob in amazement.

A broken antenna had long since rendered the walkie-talkie useless, but the batteries were still strong and evidently vibrations from our walking in the room had clicked its sensitive switch on. The simplicity . . . and implausibility . . . of the solution to the problem of the mysterious noise struck us as funny, and we giggled together in the dark.

"Won't Jamie be surprised when we tell him in the morning.

What a circus life is," I laughed. Bob yawned, "Well, at least I got the fuse box labeled." We closed the door on the peaceful room.

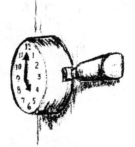

nonsense

The world is too much with me; I've begun to talk nonsense again. Did I say again? I never really stop! But when I get too busy and preoccupied and tired I talk more nonsense than usual. Yesterday after hearing the children tell about a fun happening at school I said, "Oh, I wish I'd been a mouse on the wall." The children registered only brief surprise and made no comment; they've come to expect such remarks from me. But I visualized in my mind's eye a mouse clinging precariously to a wall while straining to look over his shoulder at the happenings below, and I had a private chuckle for myself.

The children and I learned long ago that I have a private little vocabulary of my own. We discovered that when I say "maybe" I mean "yes," that "I'll think about it" means "probably," that a quick "no" usually means "I'll think about it," and "I doubt it" means "no." This translation is fairly standard, and we take it in stride. But translating nonsense is a little more difficult. A remark like, "Put the door out and close the cat" is easily understood, but when I'm really preoccupied I say some startling things. One day I surprised Leslie by telling her, "I'm going to eat you at 5 o'clock." What I meant was, "Supper is at five." Jamie had a little trouble deciphering, "Put your feet on," but of course soon realized that I was saying, "Put your shoes on." And even I had to stop and think when I told Stephanie, "If you practice your homework before you write your piano then you'll be ready for bed before you go to school." Actually we never did figure that one out.

I suppose it isn't serious that I have this weakness. Actually we all find it rather interesting when I say at breakfast, "Hurry up and drink your dinner or you'll miss the bus," but I'm a little worried because I'm afraid my weakness may be catching. The other afternoon Jamie, who was on his way out to play, called from the doorway, "Goodnight, Mama."

"Goodnight," I answered cheerfully. He stopped in surprise and listened back to hear what he had said and then grinned and said, "Mama, you know what I mean."

If Jamie has picked up my inclination to talk nonsense that means the rest of the family could too. Five people talking nonsense could make for a chaotic household. I don't think we've got time for that much nonsense; we are busy people. But then again maybe we'd have so much fun that we wouldn't have time to be busy . . . or something like that.

march

March needs music. March stays cold and as a result the snow retreats slowly. The open pocket that has formed around the base of the old maple tree in the yard, and the tip of the stone wall that is exposed, are small comfort to me when I look the other way and see the drifts still laid against the line of lilac bushes at the edge of the woods. I will have to wait a while longer to see the tips of the daffodils that will push up from the bulbs I planted there last fall.

March does not offer us spring beyond the calendar date that says we have begun that season. The skies are brighter, but with a waiting blue that disappoints our need for relief from winter. March needs music to lift us until April comes.

Each listener would have his personal choice of song for this need. Mine is Respighi's music for the pines and fountains of Rome. Spring is in Rome now. I have not been there to know that this is so, but I have read of the Roman sky at this time of year, of the "cumulus piling into the blue . . ."* And in Respighi's music I can hear the urgency of stirring life, the stirring that will come to us here when the peepers begin to sing in the river marsh and the bulbs in our gardens drive the crocus and tulip into the sun.

If I sit long enough with Respighi's music I can lose myself in it. I can imagine dawn in a garden, a garden filled with the "pink and purple of almond and judas trees."* There is a fountain there and birds and a stone seat set on a mosaic pathway. The garden is enclosed by a wall of honey-colored stone, a wall trailing ivy and new roses. I can imagine being there when the wall was new and the road beyond it was traveled by citizens of Rome: publicans and their slaves, plebians, and even legionnaires.

As I listen the music announces the legionnaires, coming up the road into the peace of the dawn. The rush of their marching feet overshadows the calling of the early birds. They have made an early start from their barracks in the city. Where are they bound, I wonder? To outer Gaul, to Illyricum, to Syria? In their busy-ness they miss the morning, and standing behind the garden wall I am caught up in the force of their passing.But they pass, and I am released back into "this beautiful house of sensation in which we live."* I am left with bird song and the moist music of the fountain.

And, as the music ends, I am left with March in Maine. But I have rested from snow and cold winds. I have been away. I have been out of myself. I am refreshed. March needs music.

*Elizabeth Bowen, *A Time In Rome*, Alfred A. Knopf, 1960

a sunday drive

On Sunday afternoon we took a ride that brought us, by chance, to Portland, where I grew up.

"My old neighborhood isn't far from here," I said to Bob. "Let's drive through it. I'd enjoy seeing it again and showing the children where I lived."

"Do you mean we'll see where you lived when you played on the Elephant Rock and Doris was your friend and you had firecrackers on the Fourth of July?" asked Stephanie. The children have heard many stories about my childhood.

The highway we followed led away from the heart of the city and as, here and there, I noticed a familiar landmark, my memories spiraled down upon the old neighborhood. We passed through a section where I remembered there had been an ice house to which we had come once a week to buy a piece of ice for our ice box. I remembered how dim and cool it had been in the low, wooden building where the ice was packed in sawdust, and how we children had scrambled for flying chips when the ice man chopped away the block of ice Dad had asked for. We had carried it home on the bumper of the car, hurrying to get it to the ice box before too much of it melted.

"Watch for Maine Avenue," I told the children. "That was the name of the street we lived on." I wondered if we would find it. It seemed almost that we were looking for a legendary place, for over the years my memories of our neighborhood have taken on a storybook quality. But Maine Avenue was still there as was the little store on the corner where we had come to spend our pennies for licorice or Mary Janes or little wax bottles filled with sweet, colored syrup. Going to the store had been an adventure, not only because to have a penny to spend was unusual, but because the walk took us beyond the safe haven of our neighborhood where we knew everyone by name and could assign every house and field and garden to its owner. To get to the store we had to pass the houses of people we didn't know, people who had strange dogs that were apt to bark at our heels, and even strange children.

Bob turned onto Maine Avenue, and we rode straight into my past. There had been more woods and fields on the street when I was a child, but its basic flavor was the same. Here were houses with dormer windows and front porches. They were the kind of houses that had attics, and thirty years ago there had been a coal bin in every cellar. The coal bins were gone, I felt sure, as were ice boxes and console radios like the one we had had and with which I had associated the voice of Franklin Delano Roosevelt. But I wondered if there were still bathtubs with feet in the bathrooms and crocheted curtain pulls on the bedroom window sashes.

"Perry School is along here somewhere," I told the children. We saw it, square and brick, just as I remembered it. "That's where I started school. On rainy days when we couldn't go out for recess we marched in the halls, and in the spring we girls played ball against that end wall where there aren't any windows. We couldn't play at home because our houses were clapboarded and the balls caught on the narrow boards." I remembered our chant:

One-sies, two-sies,
Left hand, right hand,
Left foot, right foot,
Turn around, touch the ground.

"But where is your house?" Jamie asked.

"Not far from here. That's where Mrs. Moore lived. I see someone has built a house in her field. And there's where we lived. Oh my, it looks so small." A flood of memories overwhelmed me as I looked at the little, white house. "This is where we lived when we had our canary, Sonny Boy. When he died we had a funeral and buried him in the back yard."

"Where's the Elephant Rock?" asked Leslie.

"In the woods there, away out beyond the house. We crossed that big field. It's hard to believe the field is still here; I would have expected it to be turned into a housing development." It had seemed like a very long trip through the field and the woods to the Elephant Rock, but we felt it had been worth our trouble when we climbed the great rock and found ourselves looking into the tops of the tall pines that grew all around it. I thought about the sound of the wind in those tree tops.

Seeing some boys coming along Maine Avenue brought me back to the present.

"Do you suppose those boys know about the Elephant Rock?" I wondered. "I'd like to ask them." But I didn't.

We turned the car and headed back as we had come. As we went I pointed out other landmarks.

"An old man lived in that house. We were afraid of him because he was very old, and he never smiled at us. And somewhere along here, in one of these tall trees, your Uncle John built a tree house. I went up in it one day when I was alone, and I was afraid to climb back down." I remembered how at last I had laid down on my stomach on the floor of the tree house, dangling my legs over the edge, searching for a foothold down with my feet. The air had felt cold on the back of my legs.

We passed a gathering of children, a rag-taggle group of all ages and sizes companioned by two or three dogs. From their animated conversation together I guessed that they were hatching some kind of plan.

"You know," I said to Bob. "There's a lot said today about how kids have expensive toys and spend too much time in front of the television, but I think those kids there have the same kind of fun we did. We made our own fun. We always had a camp in the woods, or someone had built a tree house, or we went exploring or berrying. At night after supper we got together and played Kick-the-Can or Dodge Ball or Hide and Seek. We must have had bicycles and other toys, but I don't remember them."

"Kids don't change," said Bob.

"I know. We've seen that with our own, but some kids never get a chance to use their imagination. They're too organized. They have too much supervision. It's nice to see that this old neighborhood and the kids living here now haven't changed too much."

The gathering of children on the sidewalk broke into a run, the big boys in the lead, the smaller children following behind.

"Do you suppose they are going to the Elephant Rock?" Jamie asked.

"Yes," was my reply. "I think they are."

earth day

Yesterday I wrote a letter. Today I made six copies of it and mailed them to The Carling Brewing Company, The Narragansett Beer Company, The National Brewing Company, Schlitz Beer Company, Anheuser Busch Incorporated, and The Jacob Ruppert Company. This is what the letter said:

April 22, 1970
EARTH DAY

Gentlemen:

We went out along our road today with a wheelbarrow and a wagon to pick up trash. Because ours is a country road people driving by feel free to toss trash out of their car windows. We picked up candy wrappers, cigarette packages, potato chip bags, and ice cream dishes, but mostly we picked up beer cans and bottles. We filled eight 30 gallon trash barrels, and we only scratched the surface of what needs to be done. Standing with our arms full of cans we looked into thickets of thorn bushes, down steep bankings and far into clumps of pine trees to see many more cans which were out of our reach. And as we walked on the edge of the road picking up trash that lay on the surface of the matted, yellow grass, we realized that most of the hummocks we stepped on were last summer's leavings of cans and bottles hidden under the grass. We felt discouraged, but our spirits really sagged when we drove to the dump, for along the edges of every road we traveled were more beer cans and bottles ... hundreds of them.

We are writing to you, as a producer of beer, because we feel that if this littering of the roadways of America is to stop you and your fellow producers must assume a large part of the responsibility for stopping it. It is going to be difficult to educate people to stop throwing their trash along country roads, but perhaps a concerted anti-litter campaign will reach them . . . eventually. Because you sell the product it does not seem unfair to ask you to shoulder this burden.

Couldn't you use some of your advertising time and space to urge people not to litter the countryside? Or perhaps you could institute an anti-litter program for school children, not only because they would pass the information, and pressure, along to their parents, but because they will be the adults of tomorrow. Or perhaps the answer is to resume the practice of reusing bottles so that the public would have the incentive of collecting the two cent deposit upon returning an empty container to the store. We realize the inconvenience and expense of all of these solutions, but the alternate price we all pay: an ugly environment, seems far greater.

Summer is coming. On warm evenings at dusk we will sit on our porch to enjoy the evening. In the half light we will look across the lawn to see the bright flowers in the garden. We will smell the scent of the tall pine trees that stand at the edge of the yard, and beyond them in the woods we will hear the owl talking to the coming night.

We will also hear, as we sit on the porch, cars driving by on the road and often as they pass we will hear the sharp clink of a beer can or bottle landing on the shoulder of the road. "There goes another beer can," we will say to one another, and we will feel discouraged. We want to see daisies, Indian paint brush, and buttercups along the road, not beer cans. Because we feel that you agree with us, we urge you to think about what you as a producer can do about this ugly problem.

Sincerely,
Mrs. Robert Butler
Leslie Butler, Age 12
Stephanie Butler, Age 10
James Butler, Age 8

We all signed the letter. The children did so with the obvious feeling that they had met a problem and dealt with it, and it was necessary for me to explain to them that the letters would probably bring very little results.

"These letters are going to serve as a very small prod to the consciences of these companies," I said. "If families all over the country did this it might have an effect on company policy, but to get one letter like this from one family is going to mean very little."

Picking up the beer cans and bottles was unpleasant work. As we moved down the road finding cans full of ants, draining rain water out of bottles before we put them in the wheelbarrow, picking up what we could of broken bottles, the children had become more and more disgusted.

"Oh, this is gross," said Leslie in the vernacular of her generation.

"What's the matter with people?" asked Stephanie.

"It's enough to make you sick; isn't it enough to make you stop?" said Jamie, quoting an ad he's seen on television. And I found myself wondering what kind of people throw their waste along the road and how they could be persuaded to stop.

There are no easy answers. Educating children . . . the innocents of society . . . would help, family efforts like ours would help, but mostly I think returnable bottles are the answer. I think back to my own childhood when empty bottles were worth two cents. Such bottles were still tossed by the roadside, but children made their candy and movie money scouring the countryside for them.

Returnable bottles would also alleviate another problem. I wonder just how long it will be before we run out of dumping space? Aluminum will not rust and disintegrate the way the old tin cans would, so even taking such trash to the dump is only a stop-gap measure. There has got to be another answer.

But in the meantime we each must do what we can to deal with the problem. Carrying eight barrels full of cans to the dump once or twice a year and writing letters to beer companies may not amount to much, but we do it because it is all we can do.

mary slack

Mary Slack's house is in Pennsylvania and so is her grave. It is spring there now and fat robins must be in the fields and tulips must be pushing their mauve-tipped leaves above the ground. In November when I was there the cornfields, which surround the house, were cut to a brown stubble, and the fruit on the thorn apple trees, which line the road to the graveyard, had been blackened and shriveled by frost. Young Kathy took me to the graveyard, knowing that I am interested in such things. We rode bicycles up a narrow country road bordered by gentle bankings which were covered with the ever green leaves of common periwinkle. The graveyard sat on a rise of land. It was overgrown with vines and blackberry canes which had obscured the remains of the stone wall that had once enclosed it. Only children exploring the underbrush would have discovered the hillock's burden.

The stones were obscured too. Only three were visible. One marked the grave of a minister who was buried in 1767. Another was for his wife. The third stone was smaller, stood upright, was surprisingly white (considering its age), and was severe in its simplicity. It was marked "MARY SLACK, 1762-1848." There was no epitaph.

"What a beautiful stone," I remarked, crouching before it. "And what a quaint name: Mary Slack."

"That's supposed to be her house," said Kathy. I stood and looked where she was pointing and in the distance saw a house standing near the road. It was strangely out of proportion, too tall for its size, and even at a distance I could see that it was deserted and a ruin.

"Let's go down," I said, and we did.

The house was very old and its mode of construction, visible where the wooden siding had fallen away, was unfamiliar to me. Field stones, bricks and mortar were used between the wooden studs. The timbers of the house were rough hewn. There was no cellar under it, just a crawl space. The house looked ungainly because someone had raised the original roof to gain a second floor.

PAGES FROM A JOURNAL

One side of the house was gone, and we looked in upon the simple interior. There was a small fireplace with a one flue chimney. The lintel above the hearth was smoke blackened and hand hewn. In the corner a primitive stairway spiraled to the second floor room which originally must have been a low loft under the rafters. In another corner of the main room was a simple built-in cupboard with plain doors on the lower half. The two windows of the house were gone, but the door was intact and was closed. Its stone step was still in place. An ancient cherry tree stood by the doorway. Beyond the house stretched the fields; cornfields harvested and waiting for the winter, visited by swooping mockingbirds, strutting pheasant, and probably a fox or two at night.

The house was old enough so that it could have been Mary Slack's, and accepting this local legend as fact, I tried to picture her there. Because of the spare inscription on her stone I could only imagine her as an old woman living alone in her small house. And because winter was coming I thought of her waiting for the winter, sitting perhaps on her doorstep savoring the thin sunshine of a November day. I wondered if at such a time a distant farmer-neighbor stopped his wagon on the road and spoke to her. I wondered if he told her, "Granny, it won't be good for you to stay here alone this winter. You're too old to live alone." But perhaps he didn't plague her, understanding that staying in her house was better for her than moving into town to live with a nephew or a cousin who would take her in out of duty, but would resent the care of her. If the farmer realized this he would have promised to stop by now and again, when the road was passable, to check on her supply of food and wood.

I wonder how many winters she spent alone in the house? I hope she had a cat, perhaps a dog, to sit with her before the small hearth, to sleep by its smoldering fire while winter winds whistled around the house and swept across the snow covered fields. I wonder how many springs she welcomed, and spring must have been a very welcome time for her. I wonder if she watched the winter-blasted cherry tree for the first signs of bursting buds that promised soft green leaves and pink flowerets that would turn to red cherries. I wonder if she went out to walk the narrow road to see the mass of blue periwinkle blossoms that must have covered the bankings, and to hear the sound of the liberated brook that runs under the road where it bends. I wonder if she walked as far as the graveyard where the minister was buried when she was five years old, and if she realized that someday she would be buried there.

Perhaps when she was 80 or 81 she walked out along the road, but in her last years she must have stayed close to home, content to enjoy the cherry tree and the robins who nested in it and to watch each morning for the farmer's men who came to plow the field and plant their seeds. I hope some young person like Kathy came to visit her to listen patiently to the stories she might have wanted to repeat about her own girlhood, to bring her a Mayflower from the woods or to share stories of village life. I hope Mary Slack gained a springtime for every long, cold winter she spent in the little house.

I wonder how she died, but I guess it isn't important to know. It is more important to know that she lived, even though what she was is just a name and a date on a small white stone in a neglected graveyard, a legend about the ruin of a crude house, and the idle conjecturing of a stranger.

saturday

Today is Saturday, and it is raining. It was raining when I woke up this morning and lying in bed hearing the wet rush in the air and against the new leaves on the trees I said, "Rain, rain, go away. I want to work in the garden today." I had planned a long, leisurely day in the yard. This is my favorite time of year for gardening. This is so not only because to scratch in the dirt is a joy after a long winter; it is also true because this is the time of year when the gardens are most workable. The plants are compact. They haven't straggled in their efforts to reach the sun, or through my neglect of them, or as a result of exuberant growth. But because it was raining, quite hard, there would not be any gardening done today.

While I got breakfast I thought about what I could do with my day. I could, of course, vacuum, dust, iron or cook. I could clean out the cupboards in the kitchen or I could work on the mending that is always waiting. Or I could paint the woodwork in the laundry, a project of long-standing. Or I could read. Certainly a rainy day would lend itself to reading in front of a fire.

What I did do was go to the barbershop with Jamie.

"There," I said at breakfast. "I'm tired of looking at the hair in your eyes and over your ears. We're going to the barbershop this morning." My thinking was not unique. The barbershop was a very busy place. We joined there a gathering of long-haired little boys and school teachers.

When we got home from the barbershop Bob was painting the woodwork in the laundry. Jamie went out to the shop to put a last coat of blue paint on "Blueboy," the little wooden boat he has been repairing this spring. Leslie and Stephanie weren't doing much of anything so I said to them, "This is a good day for you to clean your rooms. I'll hold a spit and polish inspection after lunch."

Lunch itself turned out to be a production because I decided to take advantage of everyone's being home to get the leftovers eaten up. I took all the little dishes of this and that out of the refrigerator and lined them up on the shelf. Stephanie came into the kitchen.

"Would you and Leslie like spaghetti for lunch?" I asked.

"Oh, boy," said Stephanie.

"Spaghetti for lunch?" called Bob, hopefully, from the laundry.

"No. There's only a little, and I'm giving it to the girls today."

When we have leftovers we eat in relays. Jamie's meal, warmed up hobo stew, was ready first. As he sat down to the table he said, "What's everybody else having?"

"Dad and I are having chicken loaf and gravy. The girls are having spaghetti."

"Spaghetti! Why didn't you tell me I could have spaghetti?"

"Because you can't. It's the girls' turn to have it this time."

When the spaghetti was ready I divided it into two portions. Leslie came into the kitchen.

"Spaghetti!" she said. "Can't I have some?"

"It's for you!" I exclaimed.

"Yah! I couldn't have any," said Jamie. He glared at her a little.

After lunch Bob went back to painting. Leslie, who in the process of cleaning her room had found quite a few souvenirs of her past and had decided to put them into a scrapbook, took scissors and glue and disappeared upstairs. I set to work to clean up the kitchen, a long job because leftovers make a lot of dishes and the dishwasher is broken. But at last the job was done, and I escaped from the kitchen to my desk in the little room beyond.

Sitting at the desk I looked out the window. It was still raining hard. The newly-green shrubs leaned over the lawn and dripped onto the rain-spangled grass. It was still a good day to be inside.

I turned my attention to the clutter on the desk. On top of everything lay a book on archaeology that I was in the process of reading. How pleasant it would be to curl up with it on the couch, to read about lost Dilmun, and then perhaps to nap a bit. But under the book was a bank statement that I hadn't been able to balance yet, and under that was my journal waiting for an entry.

I moved things around a bit, setting the book on Dilmun aside, and settled down with the bank statement. It really should be balanced. I had lost myself in the figures when Jamie appeared in the doorway.

"I wish there was something to do," he said.

"Nothing to do? Why don't you set up your Hot Wheels track?"

"Naw."

"Then get out your blocks and build something."

"Naw. I was going to work on my camp today," he explained.

"Well, you can't do that. It's raining too hard. There must be something you can do inside." He wandered away, and I went back to the bank statement.

"Is there any coffee left?" Bob called. I got us both a cup, carrying mine back to my desk. I looked at the bank statement and wondered if I should add the checks outstanding again. Stephanie appeared in the doorway.

"I thought you were going to check our rooms after lunch," she said.

"Oh yes, so I was. I'll be right up." I added up the checks outstanding and got the same total I'd gotten the first time so I went upstairs.

Stephanie's room looked lovely. I poked my head in Leslie's door. She was sitting on the floor amid a clutter of cards, merit badges from camp, and snapshots.

"Want to see my scrapbook?" she asked. She'd done a very nice job on the scrapbook.

I came downstairs by way of the livingroom where Jamie had found something to do. He was roughhousing with the dog.

"Why don't you go out and check your camp," I said.

"I can't," he gasped, as he rolled away from Brigitte. "It's raining too hard." I sighed and went back to my desk. I stared at the obstinate bank statement and listened to the noises around me. Leslie, who had followed me downstairs, was at the piano. Her playing almost obscured Jamie and Brigitte's thumping play. Upstairs in her room Stephanie had put a record on her player. I set the bank statement aside and drew out my journal. Opening it I wrote, "Today is Saturday and it is raining."

mrs. lyons

The bell tree is belling. Its pale pink, bell-shaped blossoms hang like gentle exclamation marks against the green foliage. The blossoms do not have a scent; it is the sight of them that gives pleasure.

I don't think of the bell tree as ours. It is Mrs. Lyons' tree. We bought this property from her heirs and they told us how she nursed the young tree along, wrapping it in burlap against Maine's cold winters. The silver bell tree is a native of North Carolina and only Mrs. Lyons' determination to have it here and the care she gave it brought it through its early years. Therefore, when friends stop by when it is blooming and remark about it I say, "Yes, that's Mrs. Lyons' tree."

I think of Mrs. Lyons in the spring when the bell tree is in flower and we are enjoying once again the trees, shrubbery, and flowers that she planted here. I think about what she created here in lasting beauty. This property must have been quite bare when she bought it over forty years ago. In an old picture of Durrell's Bridge, our house stands bare of trees and shrubs. It looks as raw and new as the dirt track running past the door, which was the Durrell's Bridge Road. By Mrs. Lyons' day there must have been a few trees here, certainly some of the pines and probably the maple on the front lawn that is weakening now with age, but not the bell tree or the Russian olive. As for shrubbery, there must have been a lilac or two here . . . perhaps the white lilac that is as tall as the house, but certainly not the French lilac in the dooryard garden, or the Japanese tree lilacs or the double row of honeysuckle or the euonymous. These Mrs. Lyons brought. And then she went on from there to plan and plant flower gardens, formal beds that bloomed blue and pink and white all summer, and many others.

In view of the garden spot she created here it would have been easy for us to imagine legends about her, but we haven't had to do that. The legends already existed. They say she befriended a snake in the yard, taming him with attention. They say she wore ankle-length white dresses and huge picture hats. They say she loved flowers the way some people love children. The impression of herself she left behind was of a strong personality, an individualist. Perhaps that is one of the reasons why in the beginning, when we first moved here, my purpose was to recreate the gardens she had made.

I worked hard to resurrect them, lifting and resetting grass infested plants, thankful for the discovery of grass covered stones that drew borders. For two or three years, it was a pleasure to reclaim her purpose and plan here, but I am not the gardener she was. I do not have the time or interest for gardening to the degree that she did. I have gradually eliminated many of the gardens. And I have made other changes too. Realizing that my plan for the yard does not match hers, I have made the gardens that remain mine.

The formal gardens are no longer stately. I have turned them into a riot of color and variety. Gloriosa daisies bloom beside the Siberian Iris, and I have added red and yellow primroses to the border. (They say Mrs. Lyons would not have anything red blooming in her garden.) I have moved some of her herbs to a plot by the back door and have added tansy, sage, parsley, and marigolds and nasturtiums for color, to her selection. In the other dooryard garden I have planted shasta daisies and in the spring I add marguerites. This season, surveying the gardens, I feel that at last I have them the way *I* want them.

Mrs. Lyons would not, perhaps, be happy with the way things have changed here, but at least the essence of what she wanted remains. Children climb in her bell tree and cats roam the yard where she planted the honeysuckle bushes whose berries bring the birds. The terra-cotta statue she stood in her garden is gone ... sold at auction. The fish pool lies cracked and empty at the end of the yard. And I have destroyed her color scheme. But the rich earth I used this year to replenish sunken plots came from the compost pile she started years ago. She piled leaves and grass cuttings at the edge of the woods, and this spring I cut into the grass covered mound and found rich, textured dirt. And I have brought it, load after load, to the gardens to replenish them. Of this I think Mrs. Lyons would approve.

hamilton house

Yesterday after two days of rain and with another promised I decided the children needed an outing.

"After lunch let's drive over to South Berwick and see if we can find Hamilton House and Vaughn's Woods," I said. I had only recently heard about Hamilton House, a colonial mansion owned and operated by The Society For The Preservation of New England Antiquities, and Vaughn's Woods, a state owned picnic area and wildlife sanctuary. Certainly the rainy afternoon would lend itself to the ride, a tour through the house, and a brief foray to locate the park for a future picnic.

We drove to South Berwick and had no difficulty finding Route 236 from which the turn off to Hamilton House was clearly marked with a sign, "Hamilton House, Built C. 1770." We took the turn and left the 20th Century behind.

The rain had stopped, but the air was full of mist which diffused the many perfumes of the countryside. Trees arched the narrow road, and we did not meet any other cars or see any people. We followed the road between lush fields and woods and gradually we realized that a river, the Piscataqua, paralleled the road on our right. We passed a small, yellow cottage, its dooryard garden blooming with day lilies. A sign standing by the gate named it

The Olive Grant House

"She is in all my books, here and there."

Sarah Orne Jewett

This was Sarah Orne Jewett country. Hamilton House itself was said to be the scene of much of her novel, *The Tory Lover*. She had probably traveled this road as a child with her doctor father and perhaps Olive Grant was one of the little old ladies who brought her molasses cookies where she waited in the carriage.

Not far beyond the house a freshly mowed lawn was marked as parking area for visitors to Hamilton House so we left the car and proceeded on foot along a grassy lane. Fields full of blue vetch and buttercups bordered the lane, and we felt ourselves passing into a tunnel of green.

The last few feet of the lane was paved with wide, smooth granite blocks that would have announced the approach of a horseback rider or a carriage. Stepping from the stone paving onto an expanse of lawn, we looked up and saw the house.

"Oh, look," cried Stephanie, and I stood and looked and saw that we had found a treasure of rich and promising proportions.

Hamilton House is a Georgian mansion, square, with four tall chimneys and dormer windows rising from its gently pitched roof. It is grey, its windows and doorways framed in white. From our vantage point below the grassy knoll on which it sat the house seemed to be reaching for space, and when we moved closer we saw that all around it the lawns and fields fell away, and down below lay the river, wide and peaceful, curving south toward the sea.

"We have stepped back in time," I said, but the children didn't hear, for they had run ahead.

"Gardens, Mama," they cried.

"See George Washington," called Jamie, and I saw that a statue stood at the entrance to the gardens.

"Little steps," cried Stephanie, and it was Leslie who was first through the ring of box hedge in the middle of the garden enclosure.

"Come, Mama," she called. "A sundial." It was hard to hurry to look at her discovery, for there was so much to see: more statuary, the variety of annuals planted in the flower beds, huge round grindstones imbedded in moss and grass where we walked, but I came at last to the old sundial and read its inscription:

Let others record the storms and showers,
I will count only your sunny hours.

Again the children ran ahead, passing through tall green hedges to clearings where ornate lawn chairs invited the visitor to sit a minute to contemplate marble maidens who hovered at the shrubbery-ringed edges of each clearing. I passed through two such glades as I followed the children's voices. It was a place for private retreat, if not for elves and fairies, so I was not surprised to hear the children call, "Oh, come and see the little house." I stepped through the wet and glistening shrubbery into a tiny courtyard and there was an ancient cottage, nestled under the trees.

"I can't believe this," I said. "This is too wonderful."

Woodbine creeping over the stone doorstep told us that no use was made of the cottage although its grounds were cared for. Begonias were tucked into shady corners here and there and a geranium filled urn stood by the door. There was a wide, many-paned, arched window that let us see inside easily. We saw a large room, empty except for two austere chairs that sat upon a thin rag rug before a simple fireplace. Another small side window disclosed a smaller hearth in another bare room and through another window we looked into a closet-like room out of which rose a crude, narrow stairway.

"It's a secret stair," said Leslie. Here was mystery and romance, and I wondered if my eyes were as round and shining as those of the children.

On the far side of the cottage another large, arched window faced the sweep of the river. We stood a minute savoring the view, and it would have been enough to have gone away then and there because of what we had seen already. But there was still Hamilton House so we turned back to visit it, sure that any house that stood on such grounds would be a marvel. It was.

We were the only visitors at Hamilton House that afternoon, and the hostess was patient with us, answering our questions and making comment on the children's observations. The high-ceilinged rooms were beautifully paneled and decorated with original papers, ancestral portraits and elegant antiques. Mahogany window seats were built into the window embrasures and stopping to look out of one window I saw a gull dipping his wings over the river below.

The children noticed the models of clipper ships that were on display and the doorstops in each room: crystal snails, turtles and globes. I noticed the little touches that saved the house from having a cold museum-like quality: bowls of pachysandra and marigolds set on delicate tables, and a small leather-bound book left open on a chair as if someone had been interrupted at his reading and had just left the room.

We walked through the family parlor and the drawing room, and into the wide hall that ran the length of the house. Big square doors stood open at each end of the hall so we could smell the warm summer air and hear birds singing in the lilac bushes on the lawn.

We went into the dining room.

"There are so many Chinese things here," said Leslie, looking at an elegant bowl on the sideboard.

"Many of the men who built houses like this owned ships that sailed to the Orient for silks and spices," I told her. Our hostess nodded.

"Colonel Hamilton's wharves were below the house on the river banking," she said. "His ships came in on the tide to unload."

I tried to imagine such a ship docking at the foot of the lawn to unload puncheons of St. Croix rum and kegs of molasses.

From the formal dining room we went into the kitchen. We felt at home in the kitchen with the pine tables and chairs, the footwarmer on the wide hearth, and a porridge pot on the crane. A courting mirror hung beside the fireplace and slipware and pewter stood on the side board.

Back in the hallway we followed the wide, gentle rise of the stairs to the second floor and the bedrooms. Each of the children thought he would like to have claimed as his own the room with twin canopy beds where an original Audubon print of the snowy owl hung, until we stepped into the next room where the canopy bed was huge and the Sandwich glass lamps and satin glass jars and bottles on the bureau were a matching bright blue.

In a small room at the back of the house we solved the mystery of the cottage at the end of the garden. There were toys in the little bedroom: dolls with china heads, a nest of alphabet boxes tumbled on the floor, a collection of iron horses and wagons scattered before the toy chest in the corner, and on the hearth a primitive gathering of school-children-dolls sitting at tiny pine desks before a white haired school-master doll.

"The last owner of the house, Mrs. Vaughn, collected antique toys," explained our hostess. "In 1943 she bought the little cottage that you saw in the garden, saving it from demolition, and had it assembled here to house her collection. When she died most of the dolls went to the Essex Institute in Salem, Massachusetts, but some of the toys are here." There was no question in any of our minds but that this small child's room would have been Stephanie's, for she loves dolls, especially those with neat black hair painted on their china heads and hand-made lace on their underdrawers.

When we left Hamilton House we had seen enough to make it seem almost too much to seek out the marvels of Vaughn's Woods, but we did so probably because we knew now that the last private owners of Hamilton House, who had given the mansion to the Society For The Preservation of New England Antiquities, had also given Vaughn's Woods to the State of Maine.

We found the entrance to the park easily and although it had begun to rain again we parked the car and got out. In the picnic grove there were tables and charcoal grills. We saw a label on a tree:

Shagback Hickory. Indians fermented the nuts of this tree to make a drink called powcohiccora.

I remembered having been told that all through the park interesting trees are labeled.

We followed a trail down a pine covered slope and found the waterfall of an outlet called "River Run." Standing where River Run emptied into a marsh at the edge of the Piscataqua we looked up to see on the horizon the green hill where Hamilton House stood, beautiful in the misty light.

"How could we have lived so close to this place for so long and not known that it was here," I asked.

"Mama, will we come again?" asked Stephanie.

"I think that we will come again and again and again," I said as we turned to go, leaving for another day's exploration Cow Cove and Trail's End and the other offerings of Vaughn's Woods.

the baptism

It was hard to think of dressing up on a hot, summer Sunday, but Anne's baby was to be baptized at an 11 o'clock service and because we are part of the family we were invited to attend. On such a Sunday we might have gone to the 8 a.m. service in our own church, where casual dress is correct, or we might not have gone to church at all. But because of the baptism, we put on white gloves, jackets, and ties, and at mid-morning, when the heat of the day had already gathered, we drove to the church.

The children dawdled a little on the sidewalk in front of the church. They were, I knew, thinking of the bright beach or canoeing on the shaded, meandering river near our house. But inside the church the quiet of the sanctuary received us. Dappled light glanced through the long, many-paned windows. The narrow box pews and faded kneelers on the floor in front of us interested the children.

"This is an old church, isn't it," whispered Leslie. I nodded and whispered back, "Our church was like this once." It was possible to forget the day for the place.

Waiting for the service to begin I looked at the bulletin. The words on the cover were "God Is Love." The message on the back said:

Many people think that Christianity is simply the Golden Rule in action. Common usage says the Golden Rule works fine as long as those "others" mentioned in it live up to their part. A bargain is made and a return is expected. Within the context of the Gospel, however, the Golden Rule expects no return. Here we do to others as we would have them do to us if we were in their place. In their sorrow, we comfort them; in their joy, we rejoice; in their want, we help provide for them; in their ignorance, we help them to understand . . .

The congregation gathered. We watched for the arrival of family members. Great-uncle George came in. He sat with Aunt Bertha, a small woman diminished further by her age and nervousness. The grandmothers of the baby came, beautifully dressed in summer green and off-white. Aunt Sally, Anne's mother, sat alone. Watching her face across the aisle, knowing her joy in her grandchild, I wondered if she was thinking of members of the family who should have been with her, people she had loved who had died: her own mother, Anne's father, our own Grammy B. I thought about how as we grow older the joys of life become mixed with the sorrows.

Anne and Joel, her husband, and the baby, together with three of the four godparents, were among the last to arrive. They went to a pew at the front of the church. Anne and Joel looked very young, but it was clear they were comfortable in their roles as mother and father. The baby wore a long dress and soft white bonnet. Her head, seen· over her mother's shoulder, looked very small and round. I was reminded of the day our Stephanie had been baptized and had stared over my shoulder at a friend in the pew behind us until he had felt selfconscious.

The godparents who had come in with Anne and Joel were relatives from his side of the family. None, I knew, had children of his own and even from a distance their delight in the baby was obvious. To them the child was a beautiful toy in the way that children are until you have been through pregnancy and birth, night feedings and colic. None of us understand about children until we have a child of our own to care for every day and to be concerned about forever.

Peter, Anne's brother, was the 4th godparent. He had not yet arrived. I wondered where he was, for the altar boy had come in and lighted the candles in the brass candlesticks, and the service was about to begin. Aunt Sally wondered where he was too and now and again looked over her shoulder to see if he had appeared in the doorway. And at last he came, a very tall young man, looking like a Victorian sporting gentleman with his sideburns and luxurious mustache. Striding down the aisle to join the others in the front pew he grinned at his mother across the church as if to say, "Now, Mother, relax. I'm here. You didn't really think I'd be too late, did you?" And Sally, bowing her head for the opening collect, smiled a little to herself. I looked away for I could see too clearly how much she loved that boy.

"Almighty God," said the priest. "Unto whom all hearts are open, all desires known, and from whom no secrets are hid . . ."

As the service progressed I found myself thinking about people who don't go to church, about atheists and agnostics, people who would not hear with charity the "Summary of the Law" that the priest was reading from the prayer book.

"Thou shalt love the Lord thy God with all thy heart, and with all Thy soul, and with all thy mind. This is the first and great commandment." I wondered if the non-believer thought that church attendance brought unqualified understanding, and acceptance, of such an admonition?

"O God, the strength of all those who put their trust in thee; Mercifully accept our prayers; and because, through the weakness of our mortal nature, we can do no good thing without thee . . .," read the priest, and I thought about the young people of this age who find their spiritual rest in nature, who scorn the established church.

When it was time for the baptism one of the godmothers took the baby from Anne, and, followed by the other godparents, went to meet the priest at the baptismal font.

"Is that their baby?" whispered Jamie.

"No, but they are going to promise to help take care of her."

"Dearly beloved, ye have brought this Child here to be baptized . . ." The baby cried a little when the water was sprinkled on her head. I remembered how people used to say this was the devil coming out. I wondered if those who reject the church think that those of us who support it do so in superstitious ignorance or in blind obedience born of habit, and with smugness, thinking ours is the only answer? I wondered if they would know, if they sat there beside me, what that traditional service of baptism said to me of love and innocence and responsibility. I wondered if they would understand about working through the lessons of the church to make their meaning personal. I wondered if they would only see and hear the ritual of the service, the words being so familiar to the priest that he did not read them from the prayer book but proclaimed them over the head of the baby to the family, friends, and strangers who watched.

When the baptism was over we recited the Lord's Prayer together.

"Our Father, who art in heaven, Hallowed be thy Name. Thy kingdom come. Thy will be done, On earth as it is in heaven . . ." When a hymn had been sung, and the sermon given, and communion passed, the priest gave the final blessing.

"The peace of God, which passeth all understanding, keep your hearts and minds . . ." And then we came out of the church into the sun. On the steps we greeted our relatives, admired the baby, and shook the hand of the priest. And we began to think again about going to the beach and canoeing on the river. The sun was high. It was a beautiful summer day.

the robin

Who killed Cock Robin? Jamie did with an old bow that he found in the shed and a makeshift arrow. The arrow was the standard of a small flag (the flag long since gone) that he thought would make a suitable missile. It did. The blunt but heavy tip, painted gold, proved lethal enough.

We had finished supper. Jamie had gone out to play, and the girls and I had started to clear away the dishes while Bob finished his coffee. When Jamie reappeared in the doorway, bow in hand, he looked flushed.

"I hit a robin with my arrow and broke his wing," he said defiantly.

"Jamie!" cried Leslie. Stephanie hurried outside.

"You did *what?*" I asked, incredulous. This didn't sound like Jamie.

"I thought you'd be glad," he said crossly. "It was my best shot." Stephanie came running in.

"He did," she cried. "He did, and the robin is suffering."

"Show me," said Bob. He followed Jamie to the door. The girls stomped angrily after, scolding Jamie as they went.

"Girls, that's enough," warned Bob. I called them back.

"You are to have nothing to say. You leave this to me and your father."

"But Jamie's glad," Leslie protested.

"Did you ever stop to think he may be very upset with himself and his attitude may be a cover up?" Obviously, from the look on her face, she hadn't thought of that. The girls hurried out, and I followed reluctantly.

I heard the bird's crying before I saw him fluttering on the thick, cool grass. One wing appeared to be crippled, and he beat along the ground with the other. It was a mature robin, one of the fat birds we'd seen hopping on our lawn in search of worms since early spring. Bob was trying to catch him. "Let us help you, bird," he said. He caught the bird and held its wings down in his hand. The robin thrashed about with his head and snapped with his sharp beak.

"We'll get him some worms," said Leslie. "Then he'll know we're his friends." She and Stephanie ran to get a shovel. I felt upset and didn't dare to look at Jamie who had stood silently watching, a strained look on his face. But then he roused himself and began to overturn rocks, looking for worms. He seemed glad to have something to do.

"Do you think you can set the wing?" I asked Bob quietly.

"I don't know. I don't really know what to do." On the porch Eve the Cat paced.

"I wish we had a cage," I said. "Everytime I see one in a junk shop I think of buying it, but I never do." We had tried to nurse wounded birds before, birds we'd found on the lawn or saved from a cat. We had never succeeded in saving one.

"I don't understand," I said. "This isn't like Jamie. He knows better than to kill anything. Why, you don't even hunt! I could understand this if you went duck hunting."

"Now wait a minute," said Bob. "Aiming at that robin was a natural instinct for Jim. He never expected to hit him. I'll talk to him ... he's got to understand about weapons and not killing animals unnecessarily, but I won't have this turn into a trauma for him."

"I've got a big, fat worm," called Leslie. All the children came running, and we crowded close to see if the robin would eat it. But he wouldn't open his beak. His eyes looked stunned. Bob opened his hand. The robin lay quietly on his open palm, and we saw a great, red wound on his side.

"Oh," said Bob. "I don't think we can help him. I'm afraid he's going to die."

He carried the robin to a low limb of the linden tree to lay him there to die in peace. A gentle breeze stirred the foliage of the tree.

"Poor bird," said Stephanie softly. His bright summer was over. I turned back to the house.

"Come in girls and help me clear the table." Jamie stood alone by the tree, head down, and Bob went to him. He put his arm around him and said, "Let's have a talk, Jim."

"Mama, Jamie's afraid you're going to cry," said Stephanie. I remembered how Jamie had cried at the end of his favorite book, *The Cricket In Times Square.* Soft-hearted Jim. He would need all the help he could get with this experience. I turned back and called to him where he was sitting on the stone wall with his father.

"Jamie, come here a minute." He came, head hanging.

"Are you upset, Jamie?" I asked. He nodded.

"You're going to cry," he said.

"Jamie, I'm not going to cry. And I don't want you to either." He lifted his face to me and great tears ran down his cheeks.

"Don't cry, dear," I said, touching him on the shoulder. "Now go talk to Daddy."

After the kitchen was cleaned up the girls went out. Soon Stephanie came in and said solemnly, "Mama the bird has died and Jamie is going to bury him and he's made up a poem and he wants you to come." Jamie was digging a hole in the rich dirt in the alder grove behind the stone wall. Bob stood holding the bird. The robin's head was turned to one side as if he'd made an attempt to tuck it under his wing to sleep. His feet were turned up stiffly. Jamie chopped at the ground with a vengence. When the hole was large enough he took the robin and laid it in the ground.

"Goodbye, bird," he said huskily. Every life is precious: Jamie knew that. He covered the robin with dirt and laid a buttercup that Leslie had picked on the rough mound.

"Say your poem now, Jim," said Stephanie. He shook his head, and I could see that he couldn't speak.

We walked away from the grave together.

"You know," I said to Bob. "Jim is going to make a beautiful man."

"He already is," said Bob gently.

At bedtime Jamie told me his poem, and we wrote it down together.

> High in the sky,
> Arrows will fly,
> And birds will die,
> Every day of your life.

escape

Summer is a state of mind. One hot August morning Stephanie said, "I'm tired of swimming. I'm tired of sailing. I'm tired of hot weather." I agreed with her.

"I'm tired of making picnic lunches. I'm tired of sand in the shower. I'm tired of my gardens," I said. For me and Stephanie summer was over. We faced two more weeks of sailing lessons, picnic lunches, hot days and sultry nights, and the multi-colored profusion of phlox in the gardens, but for us the summer was over.

We Butlers had a very satisfactory summer. We had welcomed it. We had savored it. We had pursued all the activities that are denied us for the better part of the year. For each of us there had been treats and triumphs. Stephanie had learned to sail. Leslie had taken horseback riding lessons at camp and had earned her beginner's certificate. Jamie had made a tree house in a tall pine, and he and his friends had had a raft on the river. Bob had managed to paint one more side of the house—not a treat, certainly, but a triumph of accomplishment considering the daily demands made on his time and energy. He and I had built a modest stone wall beyond the curve of the drive, which meant we could let the lawn behind it grow knee deep in field flowers. And I had enjoyed a success with the narrow garden of gloriosa daisies and nasturtiums I had put in along the foundation of the new porch.

We knew of the summertime pleasures of other family members and friends too. Grammy Dot had gone to an auction and bid successfully on a pair of Indian war clubs and a bird cage. Aunt Dot had escaped to her camp, and Gramps to his. Frank had caught some beautiful fish at the pond and other friends had cruised along the coast in their boats, stocked their freezers with blueberries, ferreted out prize antiques for their collections. All around us summer had been celebrated.

But summer palls, perhaps because we pursue it so intently. We become weary from our efforts and bored with the sameness of our days. And summer tends to get out of hand, as do my gardens which in August are frowsy with the seed heads of mallow and black-eyed Susans.

My final disenchantment with summer came on the day before we were to leave on a week's camping trip. I had errands to run in Dock Square so I drove into the town parking lot to leave the car. The parking lot was full. The tourist season was at its peak and facilities that suffice for year-round residents are hard put to support the needs of the summer population. I was about to drive on when I saw, just ahead of us, a couple getting into their car.

"Good," I told the children. "Those people are going to leave. We'll wait and take their spot." It took the man quite a while to fasten his seat belt, adjust the rear-view mirror, and start the car. Slowly he inched his car out of the parking place, momentarily blocking our path into it. At last he was gone, but before I could drive ahead a tanned young father with a car full of children slipped into the parking spot.

"Somebody else got our parking place," said Jamie.

"So I see," I said. "I guess he didn't know we were waiting."

"Look," said Leslie. "There's a lady getting ready to leave." Just beyond us at the end of a row of cars a young woman had started her car.

"Good, we'll go in there," I said, putting our car's blinker on to indicate a left-hand turn. At that point a young man drove up from the opposite direction. He looked at our blinking signal, but when the lady drew away he ran his car neatly into the empty spot.

"Did you see that?" I cried. "He knew we were waiting for that place!"

"Did he see our blinker?" asked Leslie.

"He certainly did."

"Then why did he take our parking place?" asked Jamie.

"Well, Jamie, I suppose when too many people are trying to live in one place, people forget to be polite and considerate. It's every man for himself. But you know, I couldn't live that way. There's more to life."

I drove out of the parking lot. I wouldn't fight for a parking space.

"If it ever gets like this year-round I'll either move away or never leave our yard," I said.

"I wish everybody would go home," said Leslie bitterly.

"The summer will soon be over and they will," I said, thinking how fortunate we were that we could look forward to that. The people who would be going home would be going to more congestion. I parked our car on a side street in the village, and we walked back to Dock Square.

We left the next day on our camping trip, glad to be going north and to be leaving the congestion of the Kennebunks behind. Our week of living out of doors gave us an opportunity to rest up from our summer. We didn't live by the clock; we ate when we were hungry and slept when we were tired. Bob and I had time to really look at the children, to really see them. We all had time to be together, to draw close to each other with affectionate pats and private jokes. Doing dishes with primitive facilities, sharing the daily chore of carrying water, and going for wood for our fire brought us closer together.

We laughed a lot and talked. We played "Fish" and "Crazy 8's." We scattered peanuts for a chipmunk who skirted our campsite, and we laughed with delight when he scorned our offering, filling his cheek pouches instead with pebbles that rattled when he scampered off into the underbrush. In the evening we strolled around the camp ground and down by the lake, coming back to our site to read by the light of our lantern until bedtime.

We felt mellowed by the warm afternoon sunlight and hardened by the cold night air that crept into our tents. We felt seasoned by the smoke of the fire we delighted in kindling at the slightest whim. One day we found a deserted beach and brought driftwood back from our wanderings there. That night we burned it in our fireplace and hoped campers in nearby sites enjoyed its delicious smell as much as we did.

Surprisingly, we were glad to come home. Coming back to our town and our house seemed comfortable. We arrived home after dark, but going from the car to the house I saw a pale object on the lawn. Picking it up I found that it was a leaf, a pale yellow leaf that had dropped from the tree in the yard.

"Good," I thought. "Summer is really over now." There would be more beautiful days, I knew, matchless days, but summer was over.

spiders

There are spiders in the field. They are yellow and black and large; the tracery of their striped legs would span the silver circle of a half dollar. I discovered them when I went to the field to pick goldenrod. I pushed my way through the tangle of pale asters and old tansy and reaching for a feathery plume of goldenrod saw, under my hand, a spider, sitting in the center of a large silver web that spanned the air between two stalks of goldenrod.

In the afternoon sun the yellow markings on its body burned like gold and the tensile threads of its web glistened. It sat with seeming immobility, and I felt, rather than saw, its eyes upon me. The spider had much beauty, and I recognized its cleverness in camouflaging itself in the riot of yellow the goldenrod made in the field, but when I turned to pick another flower and saw another spider and turned again and saw another, my admiration turned to quick revulsion, and I blundered out of the field.

I thought about the spiders and imagined for myself a little conceit: that they sat in the field and watched all of our comings and goings in the yard, preying upon us in some nameless, evil way. When the next day I saw a web or two in the flower garden in the yard it almost seemed that my assessment had been correct and they were indeed moving in upon us, but my curiosity was aroused more than my fancy. I wondered how spiders travel. How had they come from the field to the yard? I wondered if they crept through the grass or if they sprang from eggs that had been dropped in another season on the ground. And so that evening I sat by the fire with the dusty-green encyclopedia on my lap and read about spiders.

Spiders do indeed creep and crawl along the ground, but they also travel through the air. When newly hatched and tiny as the head of a pin, the spiderling releases from his spinnerets a fine thread. This is caught up by warm air currents rising from the ground and the tiny spider sails off to populate some other field or yard from the one in which he was born. A delicate but strong landing cable dropped for his descent brings the spider to earth.

I learned from my reading that it is the female who weaves a web and sits in its center. She is carniverous and lives on mosquitoes and flies. She waits in the parlor of her web for her dinner, alerted to its presence by vibrations along the maze of slender threads when they are set in motion by insects who trip carelessly on the web's outer rim. Once alerted to an intruder she rushes to the insect and stings him with her poison claws and then sucks him dry, leaving the husk of his body dangling in the web.

Sometimes the vibrations in a spider's web are set in motion by her mate, but he courts with caution knowing that she is as apt to eat him as a fly or mosquito. After mating, the female lays a mass of eggs and spins around them a silken sac. The eggs hatch in the autumn, but stay inside the cocoon through the winter, leaving it in the spring of the year to find another home in garden or field. As for the mature female, she sits in the fall of the year on her web, fattened by a summer's glutting on insects, basking in Indian summer suns until the first cold heralds her demise.

The spiders in our field are then harbingers of winter. Seeing them in the field and then in the garden and now on their intricate webs at the corners of the house, I feel uneasy. As spiders sit and wait and prey upon insects so too does it seem that winter preys upon us. Grey winter waits beyond these bright days to close down upon the green of summer and fall's goldenrod and, indeed, upon the spiders.

jamie's autobiography

I haven't done much writing lately because Jamie has been writing his autobiography for school. I first heard of his project the day he came home and asked me if I would be his proofreader. I agreed to that and have also been his editor, typist ("The teacher says we can have our autobiographies typed if we want to."), and, because as his mother I know as much about his history as anyone, his chief research consultant.

The teacher gave the children a list of instructions for their assignment. The autobiography was to have a cover, a title page, and a table of contents. A dedication and illustrations were optional.

"Are you going to have a dedication?" I asked Jamie.

"Yes. I'm going to dedicate it to Uncle Bob."

"That will please him. Are you going to tell why you are dedicating it to him?"

"What do you mean?" I took some books down from the shelf, and we looked at their dedication pages. We found that the recent reprint of the Bradbury _History of Kennebunk Port, Maine_ was dedicated to "the memory of Melville C. Freeman in grateful recognition of his contributions to the Kennebunkport Historical Society and his services in preserving the history of the town." _Now We Are Six_ was dedicated to "Anne Darlington now she is seven and because she is so speshal."

"I want to dedicate my autobiography to Uncle Bob because he plays with me and because he writes too," said Jamie. Uncle Bob has written one book and is well into another.

"Are you going to quote a poem or something to set the theme of your book?" I asked. Again Jamie didn't understand so we looked at another book from the shelf, Kenneth Roberts' _I Wanted To Write_. In the front of the book we found this "Quotation from innumerable letters: I have a friend who wants to write. If you could spare a few moments to give him a little advice ..."

"You see, this book is about wanting to write and how to do it," I explained. Jamie agreed that he'd like to have a quotation at the beginning of his autobiography.

"Let's look for something in the _Dictionary of Quotations_ under 'Life'," I suggested. We found, under that heading, five pages of quotations, and skipped through them to find one that said something Jamie wanted to say. The first one we read was, "As large as life and twice as natural".

"I'll use that," decided Jamie.

"Do you know what it means?" He didn't. "Then you don't want to use it."

We discounted many of the quotations because for one reason or another they didn't seem quite the right thought to introduce the autobiography of a ten year old ("Life is just one damned thing after another ...") Jamie became discouraged and when we came to "My life is work" he said, "That's the one I'll use. Work, work, work; that's all I do."

"Oh no," I said. "Not really. How about this one ... 'Welcome, O Life'." And that quote from James Joyce's _Portrait of The Artist As_

A Young Man was the one we used.

It might seem that I exerted undue influence on Jamie's project, but except for guiding him on the dedication and the quotation from Joyce I was very careful not to impose my thinking on his work. I didn't say anything when Chapter One, "When I Was Born," turned out to be one sentence long . . . a simple recounting of the date, time and place of his birth. It was Jamie's project, and he gave *me* instructions, particularly when it came to typing the manuscript.

"Now remember, use only one side of the paper and leave an inch margin on this edge of the page and a half inch on the other edge," he said, repeating to me the instructions the teacher had given the class.

"Yes, okay."

"And no lines unless you need to."

"What's that?"

"Don't draw lines for the margins unless you need to." He handed me the copy that was ready and said, "Okay, Mama. Go!"

I sat down at my typewriter and put a sheet of paper into the machine. Jamie stood by my elbow.

"Why don't you go write another chapter?" I asked, feeling that I didn't need an audience for my work.

"I want to see," was his reply. His avid presence made me nervous; I made a mistake.

"Can you erase?" he asked anxiously.

The words took form on the page. Jamie's uneven, pencilled script became smooth sentences bounded by neat, white margins.

"Mama, do you think I could get this published?" he asked. Ah, the thrill of seeing one's copy in print! Is there any person to whose vanity it does not appeal?

Jamie's autobiography is finished now. It has ten chapters and four pages of illustrations (snapshots taken from the family album). I hope the teacher will enjoy reading it. I hope she will be interested to know that when Jamie was two and a half he could fix his own crackers and peanut butter but ". . . I put my coat on upside down." And that Eve the Cat "sometimes throws up her dinner."

I have been interested in Jamie's autobiography, for I have picked up bits of information that I didn't possess before. I know now that when in the first grade he broke a piece off his front (second) tooth on the merry-go-round at school he and his friends were playing a game called "Jump On The Space Ship." I know that when Jamie and his friend Harvey go out to play in the woods in the winter they "play on the brooks. I walk across the ice and he follows. When the ice breaks we get our feet wet." And I have learned that when Jamie grows up he hopes to own a race car. This bit of information is the sum and substance of Chapter Ten, "My Future."

"Is that all you want to say about your future?"

"Yes."

"Don't you want to say something about what you want to be when you grow up?"

"No."

I don't know whether Jamie will still want that race car when he's older, but I feel sure that he will enjoy reading his autobiography.

edward green

Edward Green is dead. The news has filtered down through the family. Aunt Harriett called Dad, he called Joan, and she called me. Word is that Ed had been sick about a year, but not until last May was the trouble diagnosed. Bone cancer. His was not an easy death. And he was only forty-seven.

Ed was my cousin. He was the oldest of Aunt Harriett's five children. I hadn't seen him in years. There was a time, when we all were children, that we had some contact. We visited back and forth occasionally, and I can remember once Aunt Harriett enclosed her children's school pictures in a letter to Mum. Vaguely I can remember the faces in those pictures, faces that all had the same general look although some were long and narrow and some round. But even if I had the pictures in front of me I couldn't put names to the faces: which was Ed, which was Melvin, and Norman, and Wayne? I would know Nancy, but simply because she was the only girl in the family.

We lost contact because of Mum and Dad's divorce I suppose. My experience is that it takes two women to keep family branches together, and Mum and Harriett's ties were cut by the divorce.

Joan and I have been in touch with Harriett over the years, but ours was a tenuous involvement. It was too late for more than that. We didn't have enough foundation of shared experiences to build on. We did not even have memories of ancestors to sustain us, for the grandparents and the great aunts and uncles were all lost in time before we even made contact.

And so Edward is dead, a man whose source was the same as mine, a person with whom I shared a bit of life. Once we sat down to eat at the same table, slept in the same house, shared the same group of people. I look back and try to remember all of that now that I know he is dead.

Aunt Harriett lived on a farm in Richmond, Maine. We visited her there. How many times I don't remember, but I do remember one visit at least, probably the first that we made when I was old enough to garner memories. Dad took us: Joan, John and me. It was an adventure to be going off with Dad, to be leaving Mum at home with baby Robert. In fact everything about that trip was adventurous. We were to visit Dad's relatives, people who were somehow special, important, even larger than life because they were Dad's relations. And they lived on a farm where there were horses, cows, and chickens. Adventurous too was the fact that we would arrive unannounced, there being no telephone in our house or in Aunt Harriett's, and, as it happened, we arrived by night.

The way to Aunt Harriett's farm lay over country roads where few people traveled after night had fallen, or so it seemed. The roads were narrow and, as we neared our destination, unpaved. At one point we stopped at a railroad crossing, warned of the oncoming train only by its wailing whistle. The round light of its single headlight bore down upon us, and after its passing the absence of its beam and deafening clatter left a sense of loss and loneliness in the heavy dark. We went on, Dad asking himself as we followed the unfamiliar road if we were indeed nearing the Greens' farm.

"It shouldn't be much farther; there must be a turn here somewhere." I think my eyes must have been round as I peered ahead, looking for the turn, and once we'd found it, for the lights of the house that I expected to see at the end of the long road in. But there were no lights. The house was dark.

"Guess they're not home," said Dad. "Can't imagine where they'd be at this time of night."

"What will we do?"

"Why we'll go inside and wait for them."

The door was locked.

"What will we do?"

"There must be a window open."

We found a window that was unlocked. "Here you go," said Dad turning to lift me through the pale opening.

"Is it all right?" I asked.

"Of course it is. We're family, don't forget." My feet tangled in the curtain that hung at the opening, but then I was in, standing in the dim room, waiting to know what to do next. Even when the lights were turned on I felt an intruder and wondered at Dad's eagerness to make himself at home.

At last we heard the Greens' truck in the yard, and I hung back from greeting them, wondering if they would realize we were "family," and if that meant to them, as it did to Dad, that we had a right to make ourselves at home in their house.

"Well, for heaven's sakes, its Charlie and the kids. This _is_ a surprise." Aunt Harriett, large, friendly, obviously glad to see us, made us welcome and only later did she admit her sense of fear at seeing lights on in the house they had locked and left in darkness when they went shopping in the town.

All of this I remember, but what do I remember of Edward? He was one of the big boys who, because of the difference in our ages, had little to say to me or I to them. We shared experiences, but with Nancy, Joan, and John forming the link between us.

I remember that John shared the Green boys' room, while we girls slept across the landing in Nancy's room. After we had gone to bed and the lights were out and the grownups were safely away downstairs, the boys came creeping to the door of Nancy's room, intending to surprise us with a burst of noise. They didn't succeed, for Nancy suspected their plan, and we met them at the door and chased them back to their room. I remember bare feet on the old wood floors, the squealing and laughing, the slamming of doors and diving head first under the covers when Dad or Harriett called up the stairs, "All right, that's enough. Settle down now."

I remember that it was the big boys who milked the cow, their hands expertly jerking the milk in a hard stream that made a froth in the pail that seemed incongruously bright in the worn atmosphere of the barn.

"Let the girls try," said Aunt Harriett, and Ed (or Melvin or whichever of the older boys it was) stood back dumbly and waited for us to discover that milking the cow was not as easy as it looked. Joan managed to get some milk into the pail, but I did not although I squeezed hard on the soft udders whose pink nakedness embarrassed me.

On one afternoon we girls played in the barn. We climbed the narrow ladder to the hay mow and threw armloads of the hay down onto the barn floor and then jumped into it. When at last Aunt Harriett came to get us she only laughed and said we must be ready for some lemonade. One of us wondered about putting the hay back into the mow and she said, "We'll let the big boys fork it up again." And I assume they did while we girls sat in the kitchen drinking cold lemonade and brushing the spikey hay out of our hair. I wondered if the boys resented having to clean up after our fun. I still wonder.

My memories of my Green cousins seem to end there although I assume there were other visits. Long years stretch between us and although Aunt Harriett's Christmas cards brought news of her children ("Ed is a captain in the Air Force . . . travels all over the world on special assignments . . . going to Japan and countries in the Far East the first of the year. Mel is a staff sergeant and lives in Iowa. Nancy lives in Connecticut and has four children."), the news was about strangers. And now word comes that Edward is dead. I am saddened, not because I knew him, but because I did not.

the doll house

Santa won't visit the doll house this year because it is in the attic. It is accessible where it stands under the eaves, but its furnishings and the dolls who lived in it are packed away in boxes. When it was in Stephanie's room Santa remembered every year to leave something under the Christmas tree that stood in its parlor: a set of silver spoons, a bird cage, miniature instruments for the dolls to make merry on Christmas morning. But this year if Santa came tiptoeing into Stephanie's room on Christmas Eve instead of the doll house standing against the wall he would find the lovely old-fashioned blue and white wallpaper all but obscured by pictures of Donny Osmond. And I think his mouth would fall open, and he would scratch his head and he would say, "*Who* is Donny Osmond?" the way Aunt Mary did.

Aunt Mary came to visit with us last summer after an absence of some months, and she asked me one morning, "*Who* is Donny Osmond?" I was able to tell her. There had been a time when his face, his name, and the fact that he is a member of the Osmond

Brothers singing group was news to me too, but after three or four
months of looking at his pictures — his big, square teeth and the
cap of shiny, brown hair that frames his bright face — I was
familiar with him.

I remember the day Donny Osmond's pictures supplanted the
doll house in Stephanie's room. She came to me in the kitchen
where I was getting supper and said carefully, "Mama? Mama, if
you don't mind, I think I'd like the doll house out of my room."
For a moment, for a brief span of time in that late-afternoon
kitchen place I thought of reasons why the doll house should not
be moved. But it was a very brief moment in which my hands
didn't stop peeling potatoes and even as I mourned the loss of a
little girl I smiled easily and said, "Okay, we'll get Dad to move it
into the attic tonight."

"Tonight! Really? Good!" There was relief in Stephanie's voice,
for she knew how much I prized the doll house.

"Pack the furniture in boxes, and we'll store them inside it," I
told her, adding to myself, "Then it will be handy if someday you
— if someone — wants to go up into the attic to play dolls."

When Bob came home I said casually, "Stephanie would like
the doll house moved out of her room."

"The doll house? Really?" Yes, the doll house that we had made
and decorated together one Christmas season.

Stephanie was six the year Bob built it. He made it large enough
to be lived in by the Penny Bright and Skipper dolls. There were
four good-sized rooms, two on each floor, and an attic chamber
under the peaked roof. I remember how during the day we hid it
on the porch under a tarpaulin and behind a barricade of porch
furniture. At night after the children had gone to bed we dragged
it into the back hall so we could paint it and decorate the rooms.
We papered the walls with some small-patterned paper left over
from decorating our own house, and painted the floors in bright
colors to match the wallpaper. The house was of simple design,
much like a bookcase with a peaked roof, and did not have cutout
windows; therefore, we made windows of construction paper and
glued them on. They looked real enough when hung with ruffled
curtains whose rods were Tinker Toy sticks laid across cup hook
brackets. Bob and I enjoyed seeing the house take shape, conspir-
ing together in the back hall, stopping now and then at an unexpected noise on the stairway — was one of the children out of
bed?

Furnishing the house was my responsibility, and what a
glorious time I had. I found a black stove (just the right size) for
the kitchen. It came with a matching soup pot, frying pan, and

coal scuttle, and a little chrome-colored handle to lift the detachable stove lids. I also found, for the kitchen, a cherrywood hutch with a matching round table and two captain's chairs. Grammy Dot braided a bright red rug to put under the table, and I made a table cloth, curtains, and aprons, for the dolls, out of red and white checked gingham. At a gift shop I discovered a delicate china tea set to put on the open shelves of the hutch and a basket stocked with groceries: a loaf of bread, boxes of cereal, cans of soup, a bottle of milk, oranges . . . all of this to fill the bottom cupboard of the hutch.

For the parlor I bought a red baby grand piano ($1.00 at Grants), and a wicker love seat, two chairs and a table. I hung white ruffled curtains at the window, and Grammy Dot braided another rug, this one in pale green and grey to match the wallpaper. And of course the Christmas tree stood in the parlor, a tree as tall as the dolls who would live in the house, a tree decorated with miniature baubles. A Christmas tree meant Christmas presents and that first year there were baby dolls for the dolls, a tiny book or two, a candlestick to stand on the piano, and the aprons I had made.

The two bedrooms were furnished alike with beds that Santa had brought the year before with the Penny Bright dolls. Grammy Butler made new dust ruffles for the beds and braided multicolored rugs for the floors, while I made bright quilts and matching curtains for the windows.

There were times when I wondered if Stephanie could possibly have as much fun playing with the doll house as we adults did in preparing it. But of course she did. It commanded as much of her interest as it did space in her room. She rearranged the furniture often and placed new and different dolls in residency. Her friends brought their dolls to live in the house, for a morning or an afternoon.

Over the years new treasures were acquired for the house: a set of pewter plates and a wooden chopping bowl for the kitchen, a steeple clock for the parlor fireplace mantle that the children had made out of cardboard, and a miniature creche to set on the piano at Christmas-time. For the bedrooms there was a hurricane lamp for a bedside table, and a wash stand complete with bowl, hand-towels, and a tiny bar of Ivory soap. One of the last additions was a vacuum cleaner three inches tall.

But now the doll house is in the attic, its carefully decorated rooms filled with the boxes that hold its treasures, and Stephanie and her friends sit in her room listening to Donny Osmond records and looking at his pictures on the wall.

When I am cleaning in Stephanie's room I don't linger to look at Donny's pictures as I used to linger to look at the doll house, but I am, nevertheless, learning to live with her new interest. The other day I stopped outside her door to hear Donny singing "Go Away Little Girl."

It's not what I would sing to Stephanie, if I were to sing to her. But would I say, "Come back little girl"? No, for after all, she's been that way.

But I do regret the doll house this Christmas. And Santa will regret not being able to put a package under the little tree. But then again, maybe he could, for Stephanie has brought the little tree down from the attic and set it on her desk. Perhaps Santa will feel he can leave a treasure under it: a gilded mirror, or a minute pair of silver scissors, or maybe some crystal goblets. After all, someday, someone will play with the doll house again.

resting place

I have put Christmas away ... with joy and thanksgiving. I applied a Grinch-like fervor to stripping the tree. As much as I enjoyed the glow and color and scent it added to the front room I did not mourn its demise. I was happy to add this year's collection of cards to the box in the attic that holds the cards from all our Christmases past. I have taken the wooden angels, the bearded nutcracker, the miniature sleigh full of packages, the garlands of fruit and candy, and the elves dressed in red velvet from the mantles, and have stored them away in tissue for another Christmas.

I have vacuumed up the last of the pine spills, and the catnip from under the dining room table where the cats mauled their Christmas mice into submission. The cookie tins are washed and put away on the top shelf in the shed. The last of the roast beef has been ground into a hash, and the turkey's bones made a rich soup for New Year's Day. Christmas is over, and my pleasure in getting ready for it has, once again, been surpassed by my relief in seeing the end of it.

There is a fine spare quality to the house after the Christmas baubles have been put away. The rooms have an emptiness. At this time of year it is the house we see and sense, and its aspect is clean and fresh. The small-paned windows frame but seem framed by the winter day-light and moon-light. When we sit, late in the evening, before a dying fire, the lines of the mantle confront us. When I come downstairs in the morning, the half-light of early day softens the lines of the kitchen beams and melds the circle of braided rug into the old pine floor in the back entry. If ever we come close to the spirit of this place it is at this time of year when there are no holiday trappings or seasonal bouquets to obscure its symmetry.

There is, I suppose, a symbolism inherent in thinking of our house in this way — clear, unsullied — at the beginning of the new year, but I reject even that encumbrance. It is enough to have the house uncluttered and in order again and to be free to rest in it.

vacation

I thought we had escaped the flu that has been felling friends and relatives all around us all winter, but on Saturday night Leslie was sick. Sunday night Stephanie was sick. On Monday night as I put Jamie to bed I said, "Do you think you will get sick tonight?"

"No," he said emphatically. That night *I* was sick.

The next morning lying in bed while the children, who were on vacation from school, were busy throughout the house, I felt that I had had the experience before, as indeed I had. But this time there was a difference: never before had the girls taken over the kitchen as they did these past two days.

That morning Leslie came to me where I was glad to lie quietly in my bed and said, "Don't worry. I'll cook supper tonight."

"That would be wonderful. It doesn't seem right for your father to work all day and then to have to come home and make supper."

"What shall I cook?"

"I was going to make a beef stew, but I'd just as soon not have you using the pressure cooker. Maybe you could make smothered beef."

"Okay," said Leslie, who had never made smothered beef. "Tell me what to do." She wrote down the careful step by step instructions that I dictated.

"Get the biggest Pyrex casserole dish out of the cupboard. Make sure it's the big one and not one of the quart size. The meat is in the refrigerator wrapped in foil. The pieces are pretty big; you'll want to cut them in half. Put them into the casserole dish. Chop up a good sized onion and add that to the meat. Put in a bay leaf; they are in a glass jar on the shelf by the stove. Put in a little Gravy Master; that's for color. Add cold water. You don't want too much, just enough to cover the meat. Cook it in a 300 degree oven without a cover. If you start it now and cook it all day, by suppertime the meat will be fork tender and you'll have a nice juice to make a gravy. Maybe I can get up and thicken it for you, or Dad could do that."

"I'll do it," said Leslie, and as it turned out she did.

All that day the smell of the cooking beef filled the house. Waking now and again from the naps I hoped were defeating the flu, I thought it a good thing that my nausea had passed. I also thought that the aroma smelled right. Surely scent is a valid guide in cooking.

Around four Leslie brought me a piece of the meat to inspect. It split nicely when I prodded it with a fork.

"Just right," I said. Later when she came to retrieve the tray on which I had been served tea and toast she said, "Daddy said supper tasted as good as when you cook it."

"I'm sure it did," I said happily. I didn't mind being supplanted in the kitchen.

That evening I felt like reading, so took *The Head and Heart of Thomas Jefferson* by John Dos Passos from the shelf. Reading about a world where the law of primogeniture still applied, where the sons of gentlemen were taught Latin declensions, and where enterprising men built their mansions on the edge of the wilderness, seemed romantic escapism to me even though that world did indeed exist. But the life of the Jeffersons in frontier Virginia became more real to me when I read how on a surveying expedition undertaken by Thomas Jefferson's father and some associates one of the men was "taken ill in the night (with) Violent Vomiting." Ah, yes. Of course.

On Tuesday night Jamie got sick. On Wednesday he was glad to lie quietly in bed, while I wanted to sit up and amuse myself with books and needlework. Stephanie, who had spent the day before making her final recovery from the flu, was up and dressed and came with Leslie to talk to me about what they could fix for supper that night.

"How about macaroni and cheese?" I asked, knowing the ingredients for making it were in the house. "I'll make that," said Leslie. "And I'm going to make my oil and vinegar cake too."

"What can I make?" asked Stephanie.

"How about a nice salad. And I think there's a mix for corn bread in the cupboard."

Stephanie went downstairs to find the mix while Leslie sat on the end of my bed and took down the directions for making macaroni and cheese.

"Use the double boiler and a wooden spoon. Put water — not too much — in the bottom of the double boiler. In the top, over the boiling water, melt two tablespoons of margarine. Stir in two tablespoons of flour. *Slowly* add two cups of milk ..."

By noontime Leslie had made her cake — chocolate with a butter frosting. On it in colored frosting she had written "Get Well." Jamie lifted his head from his pillow to see it.

"That's nice, Leslie," he said. "Save me a piece."

That night I went downstairs for supper, and Jamie was the one to have tea and toast in bed. When I complimented the girls on their meal their reply was, "You're going to get supper tomorrow night."

"I am?"

"Yes, you're feeling better, aren't you?" I admitted, a bit reluctantly, that I thought I was.

And I am. This morning I was up to get breakfast. I won't be able to lie in bed reading today. In fact, no one will be in bed today. We all are well : Leslie, Stephanie, James, and Bob too, despite the fact that we (the children and I) decided last night that he would probably be the next one to be sick in the night. But he missed his deadline. We all rejoiced with him this morning, glad that he was spared the "Violent Vomiting" in the night.

the lesson

I cleaned in the front room today. I dusted all the books, polished the furniture, vacuumed, washed the face of the television, and polished the brass planter that trails philodendron in the window embrasure. I also polished the little brass lamp that sits on the mantle between the clockmaker's plane and the old bullet molds. I polish the lamp lovingly. It means a lot to me because I remember the day it was given to me and the giver and what I learned from him.

The lamp was a gift almost twenty years ago. Looking back I realize that I was very young. Bob and I had been married about a year, and I was just out of college. My thinking was still diffused with an academic idealism, and more than that, I believed that I was wise about people and life. I didn't know that my experience of both had been very limited.

Bob and I lived in Massachusetts then. We came to Maine on weekends to visit with his family. On one visit we noticed a new table in the parlor. It was an antique tilt-top card table. Although it was badly layered with grimy varnish, we could see delicate inlay on the narrow legs. It would have been an exceptional piece except for the fact that someone had cut two inches off its legs. But even though its value had been lessened by this tampering, it was still a special addition to Mother Butler's collection of antiques.

We asked her where the table had come from.

"I got it from old Mr. and Mrs. Snow. They live on the Mountain Road. Poor old people. They're having a hard time. He can't work any more. They get welfare, but Mrs. Johnson told me they have a hard time getting along on their check. He wanted to have a garden and sell vegetables from a road-side stand, but it would have meant losing their welfare check. So they've taken to selling some of their furniture to get things they need. I went over to see if there was anything I could buy. They don't have much that's any good, but I did see this table. When I asked what they wanted for it they said they'd like to get enough for a second-hand refrigerator. Of course, we had that refrigerator that we brought up from the cottage and didn't need any more. It's in good condition and will run for years so I offered to swap it for the table. They were tickled to death."

Bob was looking the table over carefully. "It's a nice little table. Too bad the legs were cut, but the inlay is nice and when you get it refinished it will be handsome."

"You know, Bob," said Mother. "You might go see Mr. Snow. He asked me if I knew anyone who'd be interested in buying some old pine boards. He has two and it seems to me he said they are sixteen feet long and about twenty-four inches wide."

"Wide boards are hard to find now, and I could use them someday I'm sure," said Bob.

"Well, go see Mr. Snow then. It would mean a lot to him to be able to sell them. Poor old soul." And so it was we went to see the Snows.

The Mountain Road ran through farm country once, but the fields had long since been cut up into house lots. Bright new ranch houses lined the road, each house a different color, each with a jungle gym in the back yard and a gazing globe on the front lawn. Here and there was an old farm house, but the old farmers were for the most part gone and their houses were freshly painted. Black wrought iron eagles flew over each doorway and colonial-style lamp posts stood at the end of each drive.

The Snow house was old. It needed paint badly, as did the barn. A small wooden vegetable stand stood near the road, but it was shuttered. The front yard was neatly mowed and a few ancient clumps of bouncing bet and Solomon seal bloomed across the front of the house. Pink hollyhocks grew by the small side porch.

Bob parked our station wagon in the driveway beside the porch, and I sat in the car while he went to the door. An old-fashioned round bell was set into the door. Bob twisted the key, and the bell rang rustily. Mr. and Mrs. Snow came to the door together. He was tall and spare and wore faded overalls. She was frail and stooped a little with age. A shy eagerness shone in her eyes. Bob introduced himself and stated his business.

"Yes, I do have some boards to sell," said Mr. Snow heartily. "I'd be glad to show them to you." He looked toward the car. "That your missus? Wouldn't she like to step in?" Mrs. Snow nodded her approval and her hands fluttered over her apron, smoothing its folds.

Bob introduced me, and then we stood there on the porch smiling at each other and wondering what to say.

"Your hollyhocks are lovely," I said to Mrs. Snow.

"Yes," she agreed. "They come up every year." She looked carefully at the familiar pink petals and fuzzy yellow stamens as if examining them for the first time.

"You folks grow flowers?" she asked.

"No, we live in an apartment now, but someday I want a flower garden."

"Those boards are right here in the barn if you'd like to look at them," said Mr. Snow, and Bob followed him down the steps toward the barn. I wanted to go too, but suspected that my place was considered to be with Mrs. Snow. The men would talk man-talk, and the women would talk female concerns.

"Do you have children?" asked the old woman shyly.

"Not yet," I answered with a confident smile. Children like flowers belonged to the future. "Do you?" I asked back.

"No, we never had children," was the matter-of-fact reply, and I realized that that was the way it would have been when these old people were young. Children either came or they didn't and medical reasons why and adoption were not considered. You accepted what was and went on from there and built a marriage and a life around what there was.

We stood lost in thought and thus it was we heard Mr. Snow saying as he led Bob back to the porch, "It was too bad that we couldn't keep the stand. I know about growing vegetables, and we could have made a little selling them. But we couldn't afford to lose the state money so we closed up the stand. But it's too bad. It gave me something to do too. I miss working. Worked all my life." I looked at his big square hands and could see that they knew the feel of hoe and scythe.

"We're so happy with our refrigerator," said Mrs. Snow softly. "Wouldn't you like to see it?" She led the way into the house, and we stood in the kitchen which was gloomy except for the gleaming white refrigerator, incongruous beside the sloping slate sink. Mrs. Snow smiled with pride and affection at the refrigerator.

"It's so nice having it. I can keep milk now and don't worry about the eggs goin' bad. We got along all right in the winter when the shed was cold, but summers it was hard." My mind was filled with questions of how you managed in summer without a refrigerator, but I said, "The table is very nice too."

"Yes," said Mrs. Snow. "We'd had it a long time, but I don't remember just where it came from. It must have been my mother's." She said it without regret, but I felt pity for the old people and regretted for them their situation and the system that prevented them from selling a few vegetables in their front yard.

"We don't have to stand here talking," said Mr. Snow. "Come in and sit." I followed him into the parlor, a small room furnished with ugly Victorian furniture, and it was only when we had sat down in uncomfortable rockers facing one another that we realized the others were still in the kitchen. Mr. Snow laughed a little in embarrassment and said, "Guess they're not coming in." To ease the awkwardness I said, "We're very interested in antiques. My husband will be happy to have the boards."

"Yes. They're good boards. Good'n dry. It's hard to find wide boards now-a-days."

His eyes searched the room and lighted on a small brass object which lay on the false mantle piece. His face brightened.

"If you like old things maybe you'd like to see this." He brought the object to me. "It's some kind of heating lamp." It was round and squat. The brass cover had a black wooden handle. Another brass piece lifted up disclosing underneath a mesh covered well in the bottom section of the lamp.

"You see, you pour some kind of fuel in here and light it and put this piece back on and it heats up."

"Perhaps it was used for melting sealing wax," I suggested.

"Maybe." He turned it over. "See, here on the bottom it says 'Patent — Sept. 17, '73'."

"Isn't that *interesting*," I exclaimed. "It's like a little stove." We bent our heads over it. And then he said, "Now why don't you just take that home with you." His large boney hands patted the lamp into mine.

"Oh, Mr. Snow. I couldn't!"

"Yes," he said firmly. "You take that home."

Bob came to the doorway, Mrs. Snow hovering behind him. "Did you pay Mr. Snow for the boards?" he asked me. I jumped up.

"No, I didn't. How much are they?"

"Well," said the old man. "Do you think a dollar apiece would be all right?"

"Is that enough? We'd be glad to pay more."

"A dollar apiece is what I want," Mr. Snow said firmly.

I reached for my wallet. Two dollars! It seemed so little. The old people didn't have much to sell and they must need many things. When I counted three one dollar bills in the wallet I carefully folded them together and handed them silently into the old hand.

"Thank you folks," said Mr. Snow. "I hope you find a use for the boards. They're good'n dry and wide pine is hard to come by." His hands worked the bills as he talked and then glancing down he looked at the three bills fanned out in his fingers. "What's this?"

he exclaimed. "There are three dollars here." I fumbled for words, dismayed at being caught in my charity.

"Yes, I . . ." His eyes blazed and his hands shook. I realized my mistake. I felt ashamed and sorry and wanted to undo the damage I'd done. I said lamely, "The extra dollar is for the lamp."

"I *gave* that to you," he snapped, and as he roughly thrust the dollar into my hand he said in a low, fierce voice, "I don't do business that way."

That was how I learned that self-respect is more important than money or anything it can buy. I keep the little brass lamp on the mantle to remind me of that lesson. And it reminds me too of how much I've had to learn over the years since college about people — and myself.

a letter

I have received a letter from Richard Nixon. It came in response to a letter I had written to him commending him for his recent decision to halt further construction on the Cross Florida Barge Canal. When the children came home from school I said, "Guess what! I had a letter today from President Nixon."

"Are you kidding?" asked Stephanie.

"No, I'm not kidding. I really did."

"I'll bet it's printed," said Leslie.

"Well, it's typed, but he signed it."

"I'll bet it's a printed signature."

"No, it's ink." I had already moistened it with my finger and it had smudged. After all, this was the first letter I'd ever received from a president of the United States. But Leslie was still skeptical. "Did he sign it or did someone else?"

"I assume he did because usually when someone signs someone else's name the signer puts his own initials under the signature."

"How come he wrote to you?" asked Stephanie.

"Because I wrote to him."

"What did you say in your letter?"

"I said, 'Dear President Nixon, How am I going to get my children to eat peas . . .'."

"Be serious, Mama. Why did you write him?"

"Because I wanted to thank him for a stand he took on a conservation issue."

The girls were satisfied with all of this information. Only Jamie was interested enough to want to actually see the letter. "Let me see," he said. I handed him the pale green sheet embossed with the national emblem. He looked at the signature closely and then said disdainfully, "He doesn't do cursive very good. If Miss Cadigan saw that she wouldn't like it very much." Miss Cadigan teaches penmanship at Jamie's school.

geese

I was bringing in the groceries, going back and forth to gather the heavy, brown bags from the back of the car, picking my way around puddles, through porous snow and ice, avoiding muddy spots on the lawn; places that had proved too vulnerable to the busy feet of our numerous family, when I heard them.

"Honk, honk." It took me a precious moment to locate them in the sky; a phalanx of geese, six flying in formation, one flying wide as if to marshal their flight.

"Hooray!" I called.

Leslie and her friend, Pam, who were in the house, heard me and came to the window, peering out questioningly between the curtains.

"What is it?" asked Leslie faintly through the glass.

"Geese!" I cried. "A wedge of geese in the sky!" I pointed to where the birds had already disappeared beyond the tops of the trees.

"Oh," I heard Leslie say as she and Pam turned away from the window. They were not excited. Perhaps they were too busy, or too young, to understand that the fresh call of geese turning north meant winter was over.

I was excited. I can bear the mud underfoot as long as there are geese in the sky.

shopping

"The girls need bathing suits for the youth group's swimming party," I told Bob. "They want to get them at the Mall so I thought I'd take them tomorrow night."

"I'll drive you," he said.

"That means Jamie will have to go too."

"He'd probably like to," said Bob, and he was right.

"Oh, boy," said Jamie when I told him. "Can I take my money?" Because Jamie has little chance to spend his allowance he always has more cash on hand than anyone else in the family.

It was a treat to be going shopping together, and on a weeknight too. We had an easy, quick supper of hamburgers and tossed salad at home, and then were on our way.

The traffic north on Route 1 from Saco was heavy.

"This is like it used to be in Massachusetts," said Bob, remembering our year there while he was in school. "This area is a lot like Massachusetts now." When we had first come home to Maine it had been different; still rural, still pleasantly out of step with suburban Boston. But now shopping centers were creeping in, and take-out eating places, and housing developments, and wider highways. Comfortable homes on main highways were being razed to make way for discount stores, plots of land that had been called "woodlots" for generations were being sold to developers.

"I wonder where everyone's going," I said.

"Maybe they're all going to the Mall like we are," said one of the girls.

"No. I think there's a new store opening up out here on Route 1 tonight," said Bob, who, being out in the business world, hears about such things. And sure enough, a few miles north of Saco we came to the site of the new store. It sat back from the highway in a huge, macadamized parking lot that was already jammed with cars.

We were delayed by a long line of south-bound traffic that was turning into the parking lot. Behind us we saw the blinking directional signals of an equally long line of north-bound traffic waiting to turn into the parking lot too. I was amazed.

"Just look at that. Can you believe it? Imagine coming out in the evening for the opening of another discount store."

"A lot of people wouldn't miss an opening. It's their entertainment."

"Really?"

"I can remember when it was a big thing to go to town on a Saturday night."

Watching the stream of cars turning off to the new store, sensing the urgency of the people to get inside the store, I said, "Remember what the old second-hand furniture dealer said in *The Price* about shopping?" ("What is the key word today? Disposable. The more you can throw it away the more it's beautiful. The car, the furniture, the wife, the children ... everything has to be disposable. Because you see the main thing today is ... shopping. Years ago a person, he was unhappy, didn't know what to do with himself ... he'd go to church, start a revolution ... *something*. Today you're unhappy? Can't figure it out? What is the salvation? Go shopping. If they close the stores for six months in this country there would be from coast to coast a regular massacre ... "*)

"We're all being manipulated," I said. "Our lives are being merchandized away." I wished we were not going to the Mall.

The Mall was not an unpleasant place to be. The flower-like fountain was pleasant to see, and the planters, set down the middle of the concourse, were filled with flowers — real ones. There were tulips of all colors, daffodils and every other kind of spring bulb. There were primroses, unusual varieties of geraniums, even marigolds and painted daisies, all grouped together in a wonderful, heartening array. I was impressed. And the stores were impressive too, although there were too many of them to be enticing.

We split up to do our shopping. We arranged to meet in an hour by the fountain. I felt a little like we were setting forth on Main Street on a Saturday night. Places like the Mall would be the children's Main Street, in memory, I reflected.

The girls looked for bathing suits in one of the shops that cater to the younger generation. The young girl in charge of the store was dressed in leather pants, a long brocade vest, and a blouse made of a thin material with long, very full sleeves. She wore the key to the dressing rooms on a string around her neck and admonished the girls not to take more than three bathing suits into a dressing room at a time. She seemed rather cross about the whole

*Arthur Miller, *The Price*, The Viking Press, New York, 1968

thing, and I was careful as I went back and forth bringing different suits to the girls not to allow them more than three at a time. My efforts to abide by the rules and to make small talk with the clerk did not elicit much warmth from her, but before we left she did smile. I felt better. We might not be shopping on Main Street, but that didn't mean we couldn't be human to one another.

We spent some time in the record shop pricing tapes and records. In a strawberry-scented gift shop Stephanie bought a birthday present for a friend. I stopped off in a tobacco store to buy a package of small, Dutch cigars for Bob, a treat for me as well as for him because I enjoy their aroma.

We met Bob and Jamie by the fountain and learned that they had spent their time looking at mini-bikes at Sears. And Jamie had spent some money too. He had bought a package of decals . . . furry feet and hands.

"What will you do with those?" I asked.

"Stick them on my notebook and trumpet case," he said.

We wandered into the Coffee, Tea and Spice House and spent an intriguing ten minutes looking at their stock of imported foods, incense, French cooking pans, children's novelties, posters, baskets, soap, candles, etc.

"You can buy anything," I said to Bob. "Remember when we used to have to go to Boston to find stores like this? It's kind of too bad in a way. I mean, it's nice — I like being able to pick up special treats like your cigars, but we've lost something. Everything is the same everywhere. People who've just come to live in Maine, who think they find a different way of life here, don't know what they've missed. So much is gone, so much is the same here now — like anywhere else. Wouldn't it be wonderful if Maine were really different, if Maine had stayed different, if Maine people had preserved all the aspects of life that have been completely phased out — macadamized — further south." Maybe I didn't say all of that, but we said it between us and thought it.

We were ready to go home.

"I want to buy a balloon before we go," said Jamie. "They're selling them in Woolworth's. Will you come with me, Mama?" He picked an orange balloon. It took him quite a while to count out enough pennies to pay for it. He felt important walking down the concourse with it floating above his head.

"Watch out going out the door, Jim," cautioned Stephanie. "Don't let it bump against anything sharp." Outside the balloon snapped up into the cold air of the night. Jamie reeled out a few lengths of the string he'd wound around his hand.

"Look at her go," he cried, and ran off toward the car, looking back over his shoulder at the balloon that sailed along behind him.

We followed more slowly and noticed a van marked "Security Company" parked at the curb near the entrance to the Mall. Inside the truck we could hear dogs barking.

"They turn those dogs loose in the Mall at night," said Bob. "They take the place of a night watchman."

"Really?" It seemed a crass thing to do, like keeping dressing rooms locked in department stores, but was, I conceded sadly, dictated by the times.

Jamie was waiting for us at the car.

"I've named my balloon Ralph," he said. When we got home it was past bedtime for him. He tied his balloon to the post of his bed.

"Goodnight, Ralph," I heard him say in the darkened room.

"Did you have a good time tonight, Jamie?" I asked.

"Yes," he said. "Going shopping is fun."

leftovers

Tonight we are having mums, chums, and hard looks for supper; in other words, leftovers. We'll have some cold, sliced pork and a bit of hot gravy. I'll warm up the rest of the scalloped potatoes, and the curried fruit that's left from Sunday. There's applesauce, and I'll add some corn to the half cup of lima beans I've been saving. The bread I made this morning will give the meal substance, and we'll have a hearty dessert: pie, or brownie pudding, or peach cobbler. The children will compliment me on the bread and dessert, but they won't say anything about the rest of the meal. They may not like it, indeed, they may not *eat* it, but they won't say anything. They know that disparaging remarks about the food I've prepared are apt to make me cross.

They finally learned that lesson a year or so ago on a night when I tried to serve leftovers creatively. We were having a casserole that I'd spent a good part of the afternoon preparing. Just before supper Stephanie came into the kitchen and said, "What's for supper?"

"A casserole."

"What's in it?"

"Noodles, cut up turkey and ham, and cream of mushroom soup
. . ."

"Yuck," said Stephanie. And instead of saying mildly, as I usually did, "That will do," I said, "I will not have you making rude remarks about our food. If that's the way you feel you can go without your supper." Looking back I can see that I reacted as I did because secretly I was afraid Stephanie was right.

When we sat down to eat Bob asked innocently, "Where's Stephanie?"

"She won't be eating with us tonight because she made a rude remark about the casserole." There were some startled looks around the table, but the only comment came from Leslie who, after tasting her supper, said pleasantly, "This is a very interesting casserole, Mama."

I don't remember whether or not Stephanie did indeed go without her supper. She didn't have any of the casserole, but I suspect she probably had a peanut butter and jelly sandwich before she went to bed.

Since that night, everyone is careful what they say about the food I prepare. If there is something on the table they don't like they just don't eat it. Like tonight for instance: the girls won't touch the scalloped potatoes and Jamie won't want any of the fruit. Jamie will ask for seconds on the potatoes and the girls will see that all of the fruit is eaten. They have learned a lesson.

And I, of course, learned a lesson about how to serve leftovers. I don't try to make a gourmet dish out of the bits of this and that I've saved from past meals. Leftovers are, after all, leftovers.

I am also careful to follow up a meal of leftovers with something the family really likes. For instance, tomorrow night I'll make oven fried chicken or baked stuffed haddock. The only leftover food in sight will be the remains of the dessert I'm making for tonight.

fenway court

On Sunday I visited the Isabella Stewart Gardner Museum in Boston. It was not my first visit there, but the first in a long time.

As a student in Boston I had walked across the Fens on Sunday afternoons to hear a concert at the museum, to stroll through the rooms, and to see the flowers in The Court. But that was some years ago, and although I have been in Boston since marriage took me away from the city, this was the first time I had returned to Fenway Court.

I went with greater curiosity than before, for since my student days I have read a number of books about Isabella Gardner and her palace on the Fenway. I did not make this visit just to view the unique building and its art treasures; I went also to discern what I could of the spirit of the indomitable Mrs. Jack in the museum that is a monument to her taste, her vision, and her money.

Fenway Court is forever the same due to the conditions laid down in Mrs. Jack's will which stipulates:

> If at any time the Trustees ... shall place for exhibition in the Museum established under this will any pictures or works of art other than such as I ... own or have contracted for at my death, or if they shall at any time change the general disposition or arrangement of any articles which shall have been placed in the ... said Museum at my death, ... then I give the said land, Museum, pictures, statuary, works of art and bric-a-brac, furniture, books and papers and the said trust fund, to the President and Fellows of Harvard College in trust to sell ... and to procure the dissolution of the ... Museum

I felt myself, therefore, in a familiar place as I moved through the entrance lobby to the porticos which open onto The Court. My only surprise was for the crowds of people who strolled the porticos, lined the stairs, stood in the archways and on the Venetian balconies that overhang The Court. Most of them were young, with long hair, dressed in bell-bottomed dungarees and bright ponchos. They leaned against the Romanesque pillars and sat on the marble stairs, holding hands, arms around one another, heads together, seemingly drawn by the flowers that filled the courtyard and by the music of classical guitar that filtered down from the Music Room where a concert was in progress. Behind the young people other visitors milled about — young parents with their children, fashionably dressed sophisticates and a few older couples.

I stood awhile listening to the music, enjoying the flowers and artifacts of The Court and thinking of the added beauties the place had known when Fenway Court was Mrs. Jack's home. Crepe myrtle and masses of azaleas grew about the Roman sarcophagus at the end of the court. Tulips, amaryllis, yellow and purple orchids, and lacy fern ringed the marble throne and the pre-Christian statue of an amazon. The delicate foliage of baby's tears trailed onto the mosaic floor. I wished that birds were still kept in the courtyard as they had been in Mrs. Jack's day, and I tried to imagine the place as she had dressed it at night with candles in every window fronting on the court. I moved on at last, taking the stone stairway to the second floor.

It is not possible to see all of the wonders of Fenway Court at once, for every stairway, balustrade, and window embrasure is a treasure. Altar frontals and other stone carvings are set into walls, ceilings are of painted wood and were brought from the palaces of counts and princes. Paintings, sculpture and furniture fill each room, and each room has a flavor of its own.

I passed through a room of early Italian paintings to the Raphael Room, stopping there by the little Pieta by Raphael from which the room got its name. I went on, through the Short Gallery to the Tapestry Room, remembering that this was where dance groups had performed for Mrs. Jack and her friends. Beyond, in the Dutch Room, hung the startlingly black and white paintings of Rembrandt and Van Dyke. Many of the men standing before these portraits of bearded men were bearded themselves. A Rubens portrait of the Earl of Arundel took my eye as did silver beakers and plate in a nearby cabinet. The sheen of the Earl of Arundel's armor seemed reflected in the silver in the cabinet. I stood a moment too before a painting of an Italian Doctor of Law by Zurburan, having been drawn to it by the blaze of color from a bowl of orange-red nasturtiums which sat on a table beneath the portrait.

From the Dutch Room I took the stairs to the third floor and passed through the Veronese Room where Zorn's painting "Morning Toilet," which had caused raised eyebrows among proper Bostonians at the turn of the century, was hung. Further along, in the Titian Room, I remembered that the sea-green silk brocade that covered the wall below Titian's "Rape of Europa" was part of one of Mrs. Jack's fashionable French gowns. She had felt that the material in her favorite gown was just the color she needed to offset the prize Titian, and being unable to match it had had the dress cut up to be used on the walls.

A large desk stood in this room before windows that looked out upon the Fenway, and I wondered if Mrs. Jack had sat there to address invitations for the musicals and plays she had held at Fenway Court or to write instructions to art dealers in Europe who were seeking out more treasures for her home.

The Titian Room opens into the Long Gallery and at its end is Mrs. Jack's private chapel. The chapel was dedicated on Christmas Eve in 1901, and from that year on it was tradition for private family services to be held in the chapel on every Christmas Eve. I thought of that, standing in the half light, looking at the French stained glass windows and Italian choir stalls, and I wondered if poinsettia plants were brought in for the service. I tried to imagine them there in the glow of candle light.

By the time I had seen the chapel I was tired, so I retraced my steps down the Long Gallery and found a bench to sit on. I watched the people walking by and wondered if they looked on Mrs. Jack's treasures with appreciation. Visitors in Mrs. Jack's day had not, and seeing this she had felt frustration. It seemed to me that the feelings of many adults were probably mirrored in the interest shown by many children for a firebucket that stood at the end of the bench where I was sitting. The children stopped before the bucket, peered closely at it, touched it, and seemed glad to find something familiar in that house of unfamiliar marvels.

But if Fenway Court does not always excite the general public as Mrs. Jack had hoped it would, it reaches them in more subtle ways. Even the casual visitor will come away with a vivid memory of at least one painting, having perhaps been drawn to it by a carefully placed bowl of flowers or a beam of light falling from a high window. Certainly the young people I had seen standing on the balconies overlooking The Court and sitting on the stone steps under the marble archways, were nourished by that setting of flowers, music and gentle antiquity. And then there are visitors like the young girl I saw coming down the Long Gallery as I sat resting myself.

She was about fourteen years old. She wore a long, plum-colored gown with sleeves that puffed gently above the elbows and then reached smoothly to her wrists. An old lace collar lay on her shoulders, and she carried an over-sized black velvet tam and a shabby brown jacket. I wondered where she had found the dress, but while it was her dress that made me notice her, it was her face that arrested me. Her smooth cheeks were heavily rouged and her young eyes were full of dreams as she wandered past Mrs. Jack's treasures. I wondered what her imaginings were, if she envisioned herself living in a Venetian palace. I wondered what the flamboyant Mrs. Jack would have thought of this young visitor and what she might have said to her had she been there. But of course Mrs. Jack *was* there and speaking to the girl through the atmosphere of the palace she had created in a mundane world.

projects

I had forgotten how exciting it is around here when school is out. During the course of the school year when I am at home alone and free to spend my days in firm commitment to some work project or in aimless puttering and thinking, I forget how it is when the children are at home. I forget how they order my days with their projects and presence.

Their presence is enough to make the difference — their comings and goings, their voices in the next room — but there are Projects. Jamie and his friends build new tree houses or reconstruct old ones. They also repair boats and putter with lawn mowers and when I'm firm Jamie mows a bit of lawn. The girls are more casual with their time, not staying too long with an involvement or taking it as seriously. They gather with their friends around the piano to make music. They sew a little on a pair of shorts that might be ready to wear before fall. Unless, of course, they are cooking.

Cooking requires more concentration, although not to the degree it did last summer, when a cookie making project involving two girls — one of mine and a friend — was carried out with a careful division of labor. ("You do one egg and I'll do the other." Silence. "Now I'll put my egg in." Another, longer silence, followed by the remark, "You're scared of eggs aren't you.") The girls don't cook that way this summer. No one is afraid of eggs anymore, but more than that, no one really wants to make cookies.

This year they make things like Banana Boats. I didn't sit in the next room and listen in on this project. I went into the kitchen to watch because I didn't know what a Banana Boat was. It turned out to be a banana hollowed out down the middle, stuffed with miniature marshmallows and chocolate bits, wrapped in foil, and cooked to a melting confection in the oven.

Young people like to eat. It's one way of passing the time. There are always dirty dishes on the shelf, and the cookie jar is forever on the verge of being empty. Jamie and his friends make Kool-Aid to go with the cookies, and the girls, of course, make things like Banana Boats. It keeps me busy making cookies or shopping for inexpensive snacks, which are very hard to come by, or explaining why there are only crackers and peanut butter for nibbling.

When I tell them that, I can hear my own mother's voice saying to me and my friends many summers ago, "Have some nice bread and butter. That tastes good when you're really hungry." When my children groan at the prospect of crackers and peanut butter I remember how we groaned at the thought of bread and butter, and those were the times we discovered how good bread and mayonnaise, or bread and mustard, or bread and ketchup tasted.

Besides Projects the children have Responsibilities. Jamie has trumpet lessons and swimming lessons and Little League games and practice. The girls baby sit. Jamie's commitments involve me, for I provide his transportation; but, the girls handle their own affairs. All that I provide is final approval and an awareness of what's going on and how it fits in with the schedule of the rest of the family. I don't even have to answer the phone. Seldom does it ring when one of the girls isn't handy to answer it; "handy" meaning anywhere in the house or yard. I have learned to sit tight, wherever I am, for the import of the call will be brought to me.

"Mrs. — wants to know if I can babysit tonight from 7 to 10."

Not that the phone calls are always requests for a babysitter. They are, more often than not, friends making contact or making plans. A phone call can lead to a bicycle ride, a movie date, a trip to the beach, a walk to a friend's house, or a friend — or two — coming here.

Occasionally the phone call is for me. At noontime it is apt to be Bob calling to check in on what has been going on since he left for work — so he won't be too far behind at suppertime.

"What's happening today?" he asks.

"Well, let's see. Jamie and the boys have worked on the boat this morning. He has swimming at 2 and after that he's going to mow some lawn. Leslie's helping at Head Start. She had to ride my bike down because hers has a flat tire. Stephanie is at Kelly's for lunch, then they're coming back here, and tonight Steph's sitting for Mrs. —."

"And what are you doing?"

"Not much really ..."

And I don't get much done, or so it seems. I am swept along in the children's activities. I find it difficult to settle in to any Project of my own, and my main Responsibility during the summer is, of course, the children. And then too, I'm so interested in their doings, which is no one's fault but my own. I'm interested in

Banana Boats. And I want to know what color the boys have decided to paint the dory when it is stripped and sanded and primed. I enjoy the girls' music and wonder what it is that has set them to laughing.

If I feel that I could do without some of the minor crises that arise out of their activities : flat bicycle tires, sneakers that Jamie has muddied on the river bank launching the boat, a disappearing cat who turns up, noisily, in the middle of the night having been shut up in the attic when someone went to get a sleeping bag for a pajama party — if I feel I could do without some of these crises, I know that once fall arrives and the children are in school again I will have an adjustment to make from my exciting summer days. But although I will have to learn again how to order my own time, it is an adjustment I will be glad to make, for, after all, one can't expect life to be continuously stimulating and exciting.

grasses

On the evenings when it is my turn to walk Brigitte the Dog it is the wild flowers I look for when we turn along the River Road, but it is the grasses I'm apt to bring home. I see blue vetch, butter-cups, moon daisies, red clover. I look for cinquefoil, white campion, meadow rue, and St. John's wort. I am interested in the uniqueness of each flower and enjoy counting their variety, until I am distracted by the grasses.

At first all I notice is the Timothy grass. Its cylindrical brush is dusted with pollen at this time of year. Its narrow leaves bend at a sharp angle to its stem. I restrain the dog long enough to pull a stalk, listening for its squeak as it comes out of its sheath, and as we walk along the road I chew the tip which is slightly bitter and moist and reminiscent of every walk I ever took along a country road or through a meadow. But then I notice another grass grow-ing out of a tangle of vetch. This one is feathered like the tip of an arrow. It is a grain, I suppose. I pick a stalk or two.

While I take Timothy grass for granted, because it is familiar to me like the vetch and daisies, the other grasses give me pause. They grow in such an infinite variety of shapes and color. They present so many different effects. At a distance I see a pale, mauve haze along the edge of the road, or a clump of stiff shafts against the background of the sweeping meadow, or an airy swath of plumage against a line of dark trees. I investigate to see what kind of growth gives the effect of haze or rippling wave, and find that grasses come crosshatched, feathered, knotted and tasseled; that their colors are lavender, pink, tan, white, and rust as well as green. I gather a bouquet as I go, discouraging the dog from her headlong pace.

"Here Brigitte. Wait a minute."

I pick a grass that grows pale green, angular shafts along the length of its stalk and the shafts are hung with pollen like so many tan tassels. I find a tall grass that grows its inflorescence midway down its stem in a spray that looks like a spurt of water from a broken pipe. I discover a short variety that grows its seed in rich brown, knotted clumps about one third of the way down its otherwise bare stalk. Another more delicate grass bears an explosion of tiny, oval seed pods on its hair-thin branches. It looks a little like a bulb-trimmed Christmas tree. Another variety, whose clusters of hard, polished seeds shoot off erratic tendrils that look like the trailing flourishes of a Victorian penman, causes my enthusiasm to exceed natural bounds.

"Look, Brigitte!" I cry. "Isn't this one marvelous!"

I cannot name them. I have a wild flower book that has a section on grasses. There are pictures of field woodrush, common sedge, annual meadow grass, crested dog's tail, quaking grass, perennial rye grass, cocksfoot, wall barley, meadow foxtail, and Timothy grass. Such wonderful names, but except for the Timothy grass I have not been able to match the grasses in the book with those that grow along the River Road. Those that I find always seem slightly different from the pictures in the book. But that is understandable considering that there are more than 150 common varieties of grass.

If I were an artist, I would draw the grasses. I would have a sketch book filled with line drawings done in sepia and India ink. If I were a needlewoman, I would draw them on canvas with wool, for it seems to me their shapes would lend themselves to the marvelous variety of stitches. But not being an artist or a needlewoman I bring the grasses home. Brigitte goes to her bed, oblivious of the treasure my duty to her has provided, and I put the grasses into old bottles. The black glass, the musky greens, the sun-distilled lavendars of the old, bubble-distorted bottles seem to go with the grasses. And when I have lined my dry bouquets up on the deep window sill before the small-paned window I have, I discover, created a picture after all.

summer

Today I went swimming in my clothes, and it was my breakthrough to summer.

We had spent the morning around the house. At noon, when the tide was high on the river, Bob took a canoe-load of teenagers down river to Picnic Rock for lunch and a swim. Jamie and I saw them off on the river bank and then he went to find the Wallace boys to see if they wanted to go out in the motor boat. I went home to work in my garden, which had experienced its usual mid-summer neglect.

In the garden I picked dead blossoms off the lemon lilies, staked leggy plants, and pulled weeds here and there. I did not settle down to work in any one spot. This was partly because there was so much to be done, but mostly it was because I was restless under the hot sun. As I pulled errant grass and violets I thought about the beach and bicycle riding and boating. I was warm in my slacks and blouse and thought vaguely about changing into something cooler. Mosquitoes flew up out of the dense foliage of the phlox, and I slapped them away from my arms and the back of my neck. At last I sat back on my heels, squinted up at the brightness of the sun and said to myself, "Joyce, you're foolish to be doing this in the heat of the day. Think how cool it will be here after supper. Think how pretty the flowers will look in the half-light. Think how handsome the sky will be, and how sweet the evening song of the birds."

In the honeysuckle hedge that parallels the garden, catbirds and robins were rudely praising the goodness of the juicy, red berries they had come to eat. I looked for them in the rich, berry-hung foliage and noticed here and there the brittle, grey spurs of dead branches. I left my weeding, got my clippers from the tool shed, and began cutting away the dead growth. One catbird, who had flown no further away than the top of a nearby pine tree, up-braided me for interrupting his feasting.

And then Jamie came, running up through the field and across the lawn

"What is it?" I called.

"I'm going to get my bathing suit on. We're going swimming at Picnic Rock . . . Dad said we could." The boys had evidently gone down river and seen the others swimming.

"I ought to go too," I thought. "It's too nice a day to do this." Jamie came running back across the lawn. It had taken him less than a minute to get into his suit.

"Jamie," I called. "Is there room for me in the boat?"

"Not really," was his reply, and he didn't stop running.

I stood there between the garden and the hedge, a great stack of pruned honeysuckle branches at my feet, my gardening tools strewn on the grass, and thought about the boat load of happy boys arriving at the rock. I thought about them calling to Stephanie and Kelly and Mark where they swam in the river. It almost seemed that I could hear their voices ringing down the bend in the river where it runs on toward the Port. I wanted to be there.

I should have ridden my bicycle over, but I was afraid I'd miss too much of the fun, so I took the car. Within minutes I was hurrying along the path through the woods toward the river, slapping at the mosquitoes that swarmed happily up to meet me. Before I saw the water through the trees I heard the children's voices. I followed the root-stepped, sloping path and came out of the woods to the light and air and the river bank.

The canoe was tied to a tree at the edge of the water and Bob was sitting in it, a picture of ease and relaxation. The boys' boat was nearby, and they sat beside it in the grass, their suits still dry; obviously they were not yet in the spirit of the place. I guessed that their enthusiasm was dampened by another group of boys who were diving from the rock with great yells of delight in old swimming-hole style. Stephanie and her friends were sitting on top of the rock, draped in their towels.

"Why aren't you swimming?" I called.

"We have been," was the reply.

I got into the canoe with Bob intending to enjoy the spot passively. The air smelled of salt water, clean and cool. Now and again the breeze carried the thick scent of sweet fern, which grew up the slope to the rock. A grey log — the bleached remains of a tree — lay inert on the swath of grass along the edge of the water. Marsh rosemary, not yet in bloom, grew out of the grass. Here and there a clump of goldenrod, harbinger of fall, threatened to bloom.

"What a lovely spot," I said to Bob.

Eventually the diving boys went away.

"Why don't you go swimming?" I said to Jamie.

"Naw ... it's too cold." I trailed my hand in the water. It was not really cold; it had been sun-warmed.

Across from us pine trees grew in a grove. I could smell them. Their shape and color was reflected in the river and looked like receding underwater ledges of greenery. In the middle of the river the breeze rippled the water, bringing it light.

"The water looks wonderful," I called to Stephanie.

"It is," she said.

I listened to the subtle, moist sound of the moving water. The tide was turning.

"I'd like to go swimming," I said to Bob.

"Go ahead," he said. There had been times when I'd said that to the children, wanting them to know the abandon of swimming in their clothes, the joy of following an impulse.

"Should I?"

"It's up to you." I wondered how wet slacks would feel against my legs. "I think I will," I said.

I got out of the canoe and across the grass to the first outcropping of stone.

"Where are you going, Mama?" called Stephanie.

"Swimming," I answered, wondering if I really would.

"In your clothes?" asked Jamie.

"How else!" Stephanie and her friends got to their feet to watch me. I was watching myself, wondering if I dared. I stepped out of my shoes and pulled my bell-bottomed pants halfway up my legs the way Bob says sailors do when they are going to swab a deck. I waded onto a platform of stone that a submerged rock made at the edge of the water. I stood there, feeling myself on the threshold of an adventure. I'd never gone swimming in my clothes before.

"Everyone should," I told myself. "Life should hold such unexpected little surprises. We shouldn't live circumspectly all the time ..." and even as I talked myself into it I jumped. Behind me I heard the young people's squeals of approbation.

"Oh, it's beautiful," I called to everyone. "It's just great!" And it was.

When at last I came out for good, all the others were in. The boys were diving off the rock. I stood on the grass dripping copiously, and laughed at myself for not even having a towel with me. I felt marvelous; free and refreshed.

"That's what summer is for," I thought. "To break out of oneself, to live freely, to at least make the gesture by sitting too

long on the beach, by making a meal of nothing but fresh peas and
bread and butter, by boating in the moonlight, or by going swimming in your clothes."

fall

   Spiders hide in my broom in the cellarway and scuttle angrily
across the kitchen floor when I sweep. Crickets jump outside the
back door, and at night I hear them fiddling somewhere under the
house. The phlox in the garden have begun to go to seed, and the
annuals have achieved a richness of color that bespeaks their
maturity. The yard is still green, but if I look closely I see that the
leaves on the trees are tired and those on a vine of woodbine that
has climbed the lilac bush at the end of the drive have turned a
dull red. Behind the fence false dragonhead flourishes blithely,
enjoying its first flowering amid a tangle of asters whose blooming
marks the end of blossom-time for all flowers. Wild asters are a
sure sign that fall is here, and I don't mind.
   Autumn is my favorite season. During these brief weeks when
nature gathers together all of her resources of color for one last
splash before she casts it all aside and goes to rest, I come into my
own. I am more attune with the world in autumn. This is the time
of year for settling in: into one's self as well as indoors, and I enjoy
both myself and our house.
   "D'ou venons-nous? Que sommes-nous? Ou' allons-nous?"
(Whence come we? What are we? Whither are we going?) This is
the inscription on a painting by Gaugin that hangs in the Museum
of Fine Arts in Boston. It seems appropriate to think about that
painting in the fall of the year. Its colors are the colors of the
earth: yellow ochre, clay brown, primary blue, flame orange, and
in the autumn, as in the spring, it is the workings of the earth
which command our attention. We think about things we've
taken for granted all summer, for we realize we're watching the
spectacle of nature drawing into itself. The trees draw back the
chlorophyll from their leaves, plants devote their energy to the

nourishment of roots while foliage dies, animals grow heavy with fat and fur against their long winter, insects hide away to wait for spring. Nature is going away, as it were, and we are forced back onto ourselves. We plan which courses of study we will pursue, we decide which rooms need redecorating, we think about books we want to read, we join community organizations, we plan trips for the winter, and through all of this we face ourselves. If we dare, we ask, "What am I?"; but, failing such courage we at least ask, "Where am I going?"

"To every thing there is a season and a time to every purpose under the heaven." I shall plant crocus bulbs in the dooryard garden today, and we shall have beef stew for supper. The children wear bright, warm sweaters to school each morning, and they pick bouquets of goldenrod in the field and harvest acorns under oak trees. Now that the evenings are colder we burn apple wood in the fireplace while we read in thick books which have gathered dust all summer. Soon I shall bring the geraniums in from the doorstep and hang Indian corn on the door. It is time for all of these things.

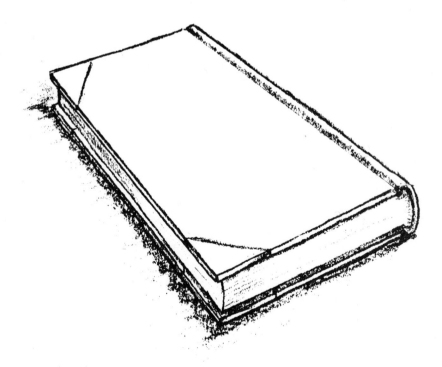

CHRISTIAN HERALD ASSOCIATION AND ITS MINISTRIES

CHRISTIAN HERALD ASSOCIATION, founded in 1878, publishes The Christian Herald Magazine, one of the leading interdenominational religious monthlies in America. Through its wide circulation, it brings inspiring articles and the latest news of religious developments to many families. From the magazine's pages came the initiative for CHRISTIAN HERALD CHILDREN'S HOME and THE BOWERY MISSION, two individually supported not-for-profit corporations.

CHRISTIAN HERALD CHILDREN'S HOME, established in 1894, is the name for a unique and dynamic ministry to disadvantaged children, offering hope and opportunities which would not otherwise be available for reasons of poverty and neglect. The goal is to develop each child's potential and to demonstrate Christian compassion and understanding to children in need.

Mont Lawn is a permanent camp located in Bushkill, Pennsylvania. It is the focal point of a ministry which provides a healthful "vacation with a purpose" to children who without it would be confined to the streets of the city. Up to 1000 children between the ages of 7 and 11 come to Mont Lawn each year.

Christian Herald Children's Home maintains year-round contact with children by means of an *In-City Youth Ministry*. Central to its philosophy is the belief that only through sustained relationships and demonstrated concern can individual lives be truly enriched. Special emphasis is on individual guidance, spiritual and family counseling and tutoring. This follow-up ministry to inner-city children culminates for many in financial assistance toward higher education and career counseling.

THE BOWERY MISSION, located at 227 Bowery, New York City, has since 1879 been reaching out to the lost men on the Bowery, offering them what could be their last chance to rebuild their lives. Every man is fed, clothed and ministered to. Countless numbers have entered the 90-day residential rehabilitation program at the Bowery Mission. A concentrated ministry of counseling, medical care, nutrition therapy, Bible study and Gospel services awakens a man to spiritual renewal within himself.

These ministries are supported solely by the voluntary contributions of individuals and by legacies and bequests. Contributions are tax deductible. Checks should be made out either to CHRISTIAN HERALD CHILDREN'S HOME or to THE BOWERY MISSION.

Administrative Office: 40 Overlook Drive, Chappaqua, New York 10514
Telephone: (914) 769-9000